YARN*play* +
YARN*play at* home

YARN*play* +
YARN*play* at home

LISA *shobhana* MASON

NORTH LIGHT BOOKS
CINCINNATI, OHIO

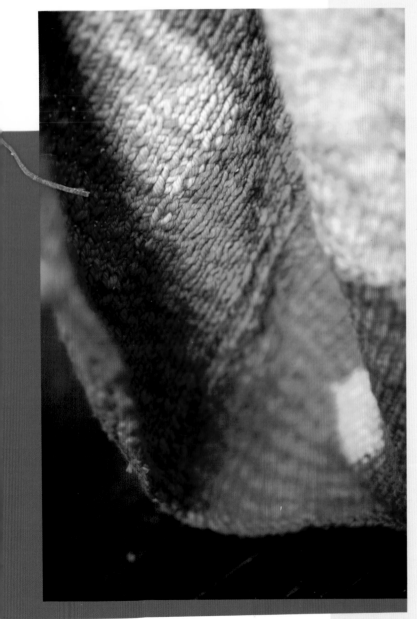

12   11   10   09   08   5   4   3   2   1

Distributed in Canada by Fraser Direct
100 Armstrong Avenue
Georgetown, ON, Canada L7G 5S4
Tel: (905) 877-4411

Distributed in the U.K. and Europe by David & Charles
Brunel House, Newton Abbot, Devon, TQ12 4PU, England
Tel: (+44) 1626 323200, Fax: (+44) 1626 323319
Email: postmaster@davidandcharles.co.uk

Distributed in Australia by Capricorn Link
P.O. Box 704, S. Windsor, NSW 2756 Australia
Tel: (02) 4577-3555

EDITOR: **JESSICA GORDON**
ART DIRECTOR AND DESIGNER: **AMANDA DALTON**
DESIGNER: **KARLA BAKER**
PHOTOGRAPHERS: **BRIAN STEEGE AND TIM GRONDIN**
ILLUSTRATIONS: **AMY TIPTON**
WARDROBE STYLIST: **MONICA SKRZELOWSKI**
SET STYLIST: **JAN NICKUM, MONICA SKRZELOWSKI**
HAIR AND MAKEUP: **CASS SMITH**
PRODUCTION COORDINATOR: **GREG NOCK**

fw
F+W PUBLICATIONS, INC.

This book is lovingly dedicated to the memory of my great-great aunt, Ruth Agnes Woods. The book is also dedicated to all my students, past, present and future.

acknowledgments

Thanks to my one and only teacher, Lisa R. Myers, for never telling me that a project was too difficult to take on.

To Debbie Stoller, Vickie Howell and Tricia Waddell, thank you for believing in my vision and for giving me the opportunity to share my passion with knitters near and far. To Alexandra Virgiel and Jessica Gordon, your magic made it work!

Thanks to all of my fabulous knitblog friends for your encouragement, support and well-timed care packages of yarn, tea and chocolate!

To my students at Hill Country Weavers, thanks for showing up and giving me the opportunity to share my insane love for knitting with you!

Thanks to Artyarns, KFI, Lana Knits, Lion Brand, Lorna's Laces, Peace Fleece, South West Trading Company, Tahki Stacy Charles, and Westminster Fibers for your generous yarn support and willingness to accommodate last minute requests and changes.

Thanks to my mother Sharon Fields for always supporting me in all my endeavors.

To Gurumayi, thanks for lighting the path.

Thanks to David Bowie for making music to knit to, frog to and cast on to and knit to again! I think I know all the words to "Hunky Dory" and "Aladdin Sane" now…

And a very, very special thanks to Melissa Sternberg for not only knitting many of these projects, but for acting as a sounding board for my ideas and for continuing to listen when I had nothing to talk about beyond this book! Thanks for always being there and generously offering your support, your knowledge and your needles. I also want to thank the rest of the incredible women who knitted many of these projects and helped me to manifest my dream: Karli Capps, Wendy Goldstein, Valerie Lanford, Debra Marvin, Kirsten Warhoe, Sara Wells, and Elizabeth Yow.

Thanks to all the amazing bloggers who have supported and inspired me. Your ideas, suggestions and comments have given me invaluable advice and direction about what to do, and most importantly, what not to do, when it comes to knitting. And thanks to the women who hosted the *YarnPlay* Blog Tour—Dana Hopings of Knitting Aloud, Lauren "Lolly" Weinhold of Lolly Knitting Around, Wendy Goldstein of Knit and the City, Tracy "Rock Chick" Stewart of Purl Jam, Jacqueline Novoselac of Serendipity and Jamie "Scout" Dixon of Scout's Swag.

Thanks to my editor, Jessica Gordon, and everyone at F+W who supported *YarnPlay*.

Jane Wells, you are a lifesaver! Thanks for squeezing the *Knitty Gritty* projects into your busy schedule of school, sports and homework while I cranked out the projects for this book.

Thanks to the everyday muses I pass on the street, women with a fearless sense of style who inspire me to push the envelope and to expand my ideas about what looks good. And, finally, thanks to all the inspiring men and women who are thinking outside the box and looking for new ways to create and craft!

contents

MATERIALS
+ TOOLS

Before you cast on, you'll want to make sure you have the right materials and tools for the project you've chosen. In this section, you will find helpful information about yarn and needles, as well as a guide to choosing the right colors for your homey handknits.

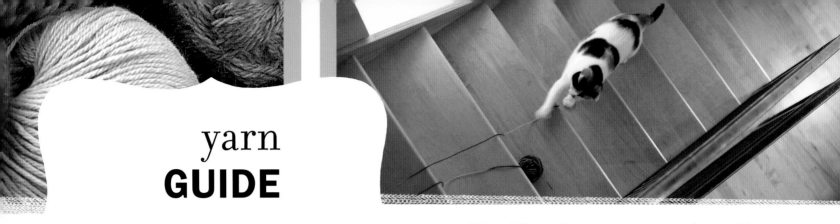

yarn
GUIDE

Before you begin knitting a project, consider two important factors: form and function. Form speaks to the aesthetic quality of the project, while function brings up issues of usefulness and durability. Is your primary purpose to create an eye-catching work of art? Or is your purpose to create a piece that can sustain loads of everyday wear and tear? While lofty yarns like cashmere, alpaca and mohair create great drape and are lovely to touch, they are also the least durable. Tightly plied wools and dense cotton can withstand frequent use, but they can be heavy, and in the case of wool, feel rough and scratchy against bare skin. What's a knitter to do? My advice is to first decide whether your primary concern is form or function. Next, take your time choosing the right yarn for your project. Finally, educate yourself on how to care for handknits. With proper care and storage you can extend the life of your handknit accessories.

Be sure to check the ball band for care instructions before you make your purchase. If you're not into hand-washing or don't want to spend money on dry cleaning, you probably shouldn't invest in delicate, care-intensive fibers. While superwash wools might be a little more expensive, it's worth it when it means they can go from washer to dryer with no worries!

ANIMAL, VEGETABLE OR SYNTHETIC

Ultimately, the quality of a piece is only as good as the yarn with which it's knit. I prefer to work with natural fibers because they look great, and feel good against your skin too. With the vast range of yarns available today, there is something to fit the taste, needs and budget of every knitter.

Before you venture into the wide world of yarn, there are just a few things you should know. It's very important to pick the fiber type, weight and texture that's right for the piece you're making.

Fibers fall into three categories: animal, vegetable or synthetic.

Animal fibers include alpaca, angora, camel hair, cashmere, llama, mohair, silk and wool. These fibers come in all weights, colors and price ranges. Wool in particular is the staple of knitting fibers, and is often quite affordable. Sweaters, scarves and hats are good projects to make with wool.

Vegetable fibers include cotton, hemp and linen. These lighter-weight and breathable fibers are great for summer clothing.

Synthetics include acrylic, polyamide and polyester. These are generally the most affordable yarns. Acrylic yarn is great for baby projects because it can be machine washed and dried.

WOOL AND WOOL BLENDS

These are definitely the most durable yarns and are perfect for afghans and cushion covers that will get a lot of everyday use. Most wool yarns can endure a gentle-cycle, cold-water wash. (Be sure to check the label for care instructions.) However, not all wools can stand up to the heat of a dryer. Only superwash wools are made to withstand both the washer and the dryer, making them a great choice for baby blankets.

COTTON AND COTTON BLENDS

Cotton is perfect for blankets and afghans that will be used during warm weather. It is sturdy enough to be used for bathroom and kitchen rugs. Items that will be washed frequently, like dishcloths and tea towels, should be knit with durable, care-friendly fibers like cotton. Keep in mind that cottons do shrink! Dry them on a low setting and remove them from the dryer while still slightly wet in order to avoid shrinkage. This

is the obvious choice for those who are allergic to wool or other animal fibers.

DENIM

Just like your favorite pair of jeans, projects knit with denim yarn will bleed, fade and shrink. Hand-wash items worked in denim yarn in cool water and lay flat to dry. Be sure to pre-wash the yarn you will use for sewing seams. I, for one, like the well-worn patina of washed denim, but if that look doesn't turn you on, you had better stick to dry cleaning! This fiber is sturdy and fashionable, making it a good choice for handknits for the hipster in your life.

GENERAL GUIDELINES FOR YARN WEIGHTS

a **SUPER BULKY** up to 11 sts = 4" (10cm)

b **HEAVY WORSTED** 16 sts = 4" (10cm)

c **CHUNKY/BULKY** 12–15 sts = 4" (10cm)

d **FINGERING/SOCK WEIGHT** 28 sts = 4" (10cm)

e **ARAN/WORSTED WEIGHT** 18–20 sts = 4" (10cm)

f **SPORT WEIGHT** 24 sts = 4" (10cm)

g **DK WEIGHT** 21–22 sts = 4" (10cm)

h **LACE WEIGHT** 32+ sts = 4" (10cm)

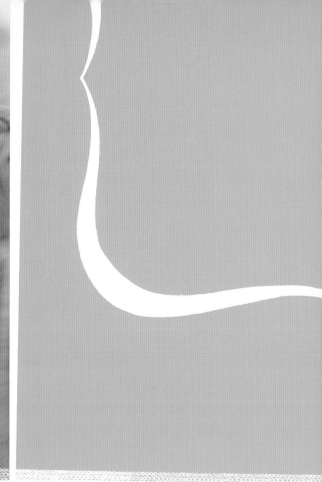

HEMP

Hemp comes from the Cannabis Sativa plant, but don't get any funny ideas—it's not marijuana! It is an incredibly strong plant fiber. High-quality hemp yarn won't shrink, stretch or pill. It can go from the washing machine, on a cold/gentle cycle, to a low temperature in the dryer. This stiff fiber becomes softer with each wash. Its only drawback is that it's a little tough to knit with. However, you can pre-wash hemp yarn before knitting with it to make it easier on your hands.

ALPACA, CASHMERE AND MOHAIR

These luscious fibers are best used on handknits that will be treated with kid gloves (no pun intended). Save them for throws and other accessories that will be used in low-traffic areas of the home. Gently hand-wash items knit in these luxury fibers in cool water and lay flat to dry. The word on the street is that nine out of ten sons, boyfriends and even husbands will not

treat these items with the respect they deserve. Save these precious yarns for items that you are knitting for yourself or giving to someone who will really appreciate them!

SILK

Silk is one of the strongest fibers around. It is sturdy, it has a lovely sheen, and in most cases it is slow to pill. Hand-wash it in cool water and lay flat to dry. It is a good choice for items that are destined to be family heirlooms.

WEIGHING THE OPTIONS
Yarn can be ultra-fine or super-thick. Or thick-and-thin. Make sure to pick a yarn that's the same weight as the yarn given for the pattern you're using. When it comes to yarn weight, the standards are not set in stone.

A HANK, A SKEIN OR A BALL

Yarn can come in a loose hank, in a skein or in a ball.

A *hank* is yarn that's been loosely looped and then twisted and tied. It must be wound into a ball before you can knit with it. You can wind it by hand or with a swift and ball winder. Many yarn stores will wind a hank for you at no charge.

A *skein* of yarn is oblong in shape, and the free end is usually drawn from its center, which keeps the yarn from rolling around.

A *ball* of yarn is, well, a ball. It's round, and the free end is usually on the outside, which means it will do a fair bit of rolling.

Be sure to choose a yarn that gives you the gauge called for in the pattern. Or you can double or even triple strand lighter-weight yarns to attain the required gauge. This is a great way to use up leftover yarn.

needle **GUIDE**

Before you cast on for any project, make sure you have the right needles. Having the correct needle size for the yarn you're working with is key to achieving the correct gauge. You may choose needles made from any material you like. Here's a guide to choosing the best needle for you.

STRAIGHT VS CIRCULAR

Straight needles are essentially long or short sticks with a knob or a flat circle at one end to keep the stitches from sliding off. They are exclusively used for projects that are knit flat, and they work best for projects that are small to medium in size. Circular needles, which are attached to each other with a flexible plastic cord, are often used to knit in the round, but they can also be used to knit flat pieces. Afghans, other heavy pieces and projects with a large number of cast-on stitches are best suited to circular needles, as they allow you more flexibility and ease of movement, taking the weight of the project off your wrists. Also, projects on circular needles are easier to store, making it a cinch to throw them in your bag so you can knit on the go!

DOUBLE-POINTED NEEDLES

Double-pointed needles (DPNs) have a point at each end, and they come in a set of four or five. In addition to using double-pointed needles (DPNs) to work in the round, DPNs are perfect for knitting flat projects with a small number of stitches. Stitches are distributed evenly over three or four of the needles, and the remaining needle is used to work the stitches. Double-pointed needles are especially handy for working small things in the round, like the tops of hats, or socks. When working with DPNs you may want to use point protectors to prevent your stitches from falling off the end!!

WHAT'S YOUR TYPE?

Needles can be made from metal, plastic, casein, wood, bamboo or bone.

Those who knit tightly may prefer the smoothness of metal needles, while a loose knitter may get more satisfaction from knitting with bamboo or wood. Also, many synthetic yarns are slippery to knit with and work better paired with bamboo or wood, while natural fibers get the slide they need on metal needles.

METAL NEEDLES are usually made from aluminum. They're super slippery, and the slickest variety can make your knitting quite speedy.

PLASTIC NEEDLES are often the most lightweight and economical choice. They're slightly more slippery than bamboo needles.

CASEIN NEEDLES are made from a milk protein. They're slightly flexible and are less slippery than metal needles.

BAMBOO OR WOODEN NEEDLES "grab" the yarn, keeping stitches steady.

DOUBLE-POINTED NEEDLES
Wooden DPNs courtesy of Laurel Hill.

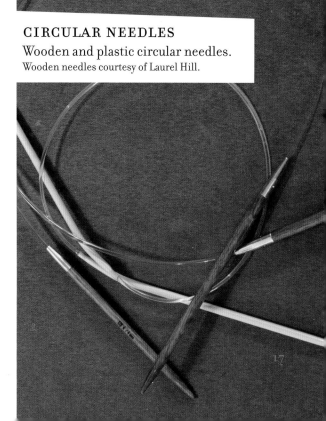

CIRCULAR NEEDLES
Wooden and plastic circular needles.
Wooden needles courtesy of Laurel Hill.

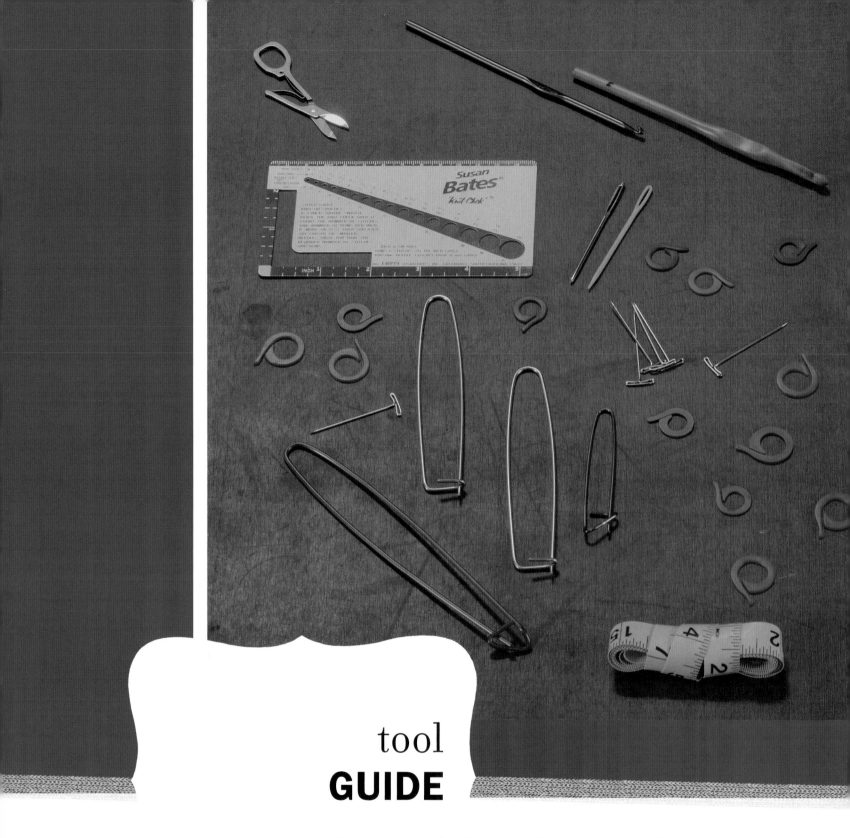

tool
GUIDE

The proper array of tools is essential to fun and pain-free knitting. Most of the projects in this book are fairly simple, so you can get away with the bare minimum. But you'll still definitely need a basic selection. Following is a guide to the general tools you'll need.

STITCH GAUGE: This is a little square of
plastic with ruled numbers on the sides
and an L-shaped cutout along two ruled
edges. You can lay the stitch gauge over
your knitted swatch and count how many
stitches and how many rows fit inside
the cutout. Then divide the number of
stitches by the number of inches (how
long and wide the cutout is) and you've
calculated your gauge.

POINT PROTECTORS: These are little
eraser-like plastic pieces that slide onto
the pointed ends of needles to keep
stitches from sliding off.

ROW COUNTER: This small plastic tube
has rotating numbers (kind of like those
on a combination lock) that let you keep
track of your rows.

SCISSORS: You'll always need a pair
of scissors. Keep a small pair in your
knitting bag.

STITCH HOLDERS: Some are like safety
pins without the sharp point. Others
open on both ends for easy access. They
come in all sizes and allow you to slide
stitches off your needles and keep them
neatly in place.

TAPE MEASURE: A flexible cloth or plastic
tape measure is invaluable to a knitter.

DARNING (YARN) NEEDLE: This is a
blunt-tipped needle with a large eye to
accommodate yarn. Use a darning needle
to sew seams together.

RING MARKERS: These little circles of plastic
slide onto your knitting to help you keep track
of important spots in your knitting—like the
beginning of a round.

RUSTPROOF LOLLIPOP OR T-PINS: These
large straight pins are great for securing pieces
for blocking.

CABLE NEEDLES: These small needles can
be U-shaped or candy-cane-shaped. Choose
a cable needle that is approximately the same
size as the needles you're using for the main
part of the project.

CROCHET HOOKS: Just like knitting needles,
these hooks come in lots of different sizes. Buy
a selection and use them to help you pick up
dropped stitches and to make crochet borders.

PLAYING *with color*

USE A FAVORITE PAINTING OR COLOR PHOTO FOR INSPIRATION.

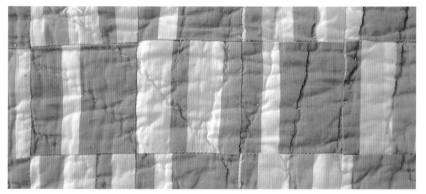

COPY COLORS FROM A VINTAGE QUILT.

EXPLORE WALLPAPER AND FABRIC TO FIND NOVEL COLOR SCHEMES.

There are two types of knitters: Those who are into intense stitch patterns, like cables or lace, and those who are into working with color. I've always fallen in with the latter group. For me, knitting with color is like painting or taking a photograph. Sometimes I'm seeking to capture a certain mood or feeling, and at other moments I just like to see where the colors take me. Occasionally, I stick with one color family, but more often I challenge myself to introduce an 'ugly' color into the group or to knit with a handful of random colors. Having a limited amount of yarns on hand can be the beginning of a surprisingly beautiful project. My method of working with color is to start with what is in my stash and then buy a skein or three to flush it out.

Like most people, I have a palette that I prefer. Last year it was blues and greens. Now it's blood red, charcoal and cream. In order to keep my knitting interesting I challenge myself to embrace colors I despise. However, I am careful not to go with colors that I don't wear well or that I'm just not ready for. It's a fine line, but one thing I know for sure is that working with color in an unexpected way keeps me excited about my projects because I never know what will happen next!

PERUSE VINTAGE FASHION AND INTERIOR DESIGN MAGAZINES FOR COOL, RETRO PALETTES.

EVERYBODY KNOWS AN ADVENTUROUS DRESSER. WHAT CRAZY COLORS ARE YOUR LOCAL FASHION ICONS WORKING TODAY?

21

LIVING
with *color*

Everyone knows color plays a big role in setting a particular mood. It can lift your spirits or it can leave you feeling exhausted and overwhelmed. The same color can even affect people of different temperaments differently. Here are a few questions to ask yourself before choosing a color to work with:

What colors do you respond to in a positive way? What colors totally turn you off?

What mood are you seeking to create in a room? Do you want your handknit piece to blend in or to create contrast?

Now that you have established what vibe you are going for and you know what colors you want to work with and which ones you hope to avoid, use the following guide to fine-tune your choices:

To give a room a more spacious feel, choose airy, neutralizing colors like white, ecru, pale blue and light gray.

To bring warmth to a room, choose sunset shades like red, watermelon, orange and golden yellow.

To cool down a room, use soothing shades of blue, green and gray.

To bring personality to a white room, accentuate it with strong colors like grass green, fire-engine red, royal blue and lemon yellow.

For drama, use bold combinations like black and scarlet or purple and charcoal.

For sophistication, use metallics like silver, gold, copper and bronze.

Don't forget about contrast! A rose-colored room could use a shot of lime or citron. Earth tones will glow when you introduce a metallic accessory.

A QUICK GUIDE TO COLOR

❋❋ **RED** represents the fire element. It stimulates the appetite and brings warmth, energy and passion.

❋❋ **ORANGE** and **YELLOW** are cheerful, enthusiastic and fun. They inspire creativity.

❋❋ **GREEN** represents nature and the earth itself. It is healing and rejuvenating, bringing balance and harmony.

❋❋ **BLUE** represents the ocean and the water element. It is cooling, soothing and tranquil.

❋❋ **PURPLE** has long been associated with royalty. It denotes luxury and spiritual depth.

❋❋ **PINK** raises the spirits. It suggests youthfulness and femininity.

❋❋ **BROWN** represents stability and grounding.

❋❋ **WHITE** indicates cleanliness, clarity and purity.

❋❋ **BLACK**, the color of night, brings intensity, sophistication and glamour.

❋❋ **METALLICS** denote affluence and sophistication.

❋❋ **GRAY** balances and neutralizes stronger colors.

PATTERNS, PATTERNS, PATTERNS!

While color sets the character of a room, patterns give it personality. I find that a lot of people shy away from them because they don't know how to make them work in a room or they are afraid they won't play nicely with other patterns. When combining several patterns, you want them to share a common element, such as color or design. For example, you could use several polka-dot patterns in the same room or you could combine a stripe and a paisley that both contain the same color. I try to avoid having my decor become too matchy-matchy. That's so boring. An unexpected color or pattern makes things pop, adding an air of excitement. What room in your house or apartment could use a little boost?

PLAYING *with* *yarn* at home

I have a confession to make. When it comes to home decor, I've come late to the party. For most of my life all I really cared about was fashion. I traveled around quite a bit, and I moved just as frequently. And when I was in town, I tended to spend more time hanging out at restaurants and clubs than nesting in my apartment. I wasn't the least bit concerned with decorating my space or even with having a sofa to sit on. In recent years, my life has become a little less nomadic, and I've learned to enjoy spending time at home. It was a bit shocking suddenly to realize that while I had a dozen outfits for every occasion, I owned precious little in the way of things to make me feel comfortable and inspired in my everyday environment. Not being in the position to just go out and buy a truckload of stuff, I had to get creative. First, I made a decision about which things I could compromise on and which I could not. In regard to the latter, I decided it was worthwhile to spend the money on a sofa that I really loved. I was willing to improvise on just about everything else. Today I live in a warm and inviting space that combines a couple of must-have new pieces with loads of vintage finds, all complemented by unique, handknit accessories. Mixing different elements like new and vintage, store-bought and handmade, and a tasteful blend of kitschy and modern gives my space a feeling of vibrancy and warmth.

I've always sought to maintain a personal look that is both unique and stylish, and I now apply that same attitude to my home decor. I aim to keep things flexible and fresh. Home accessories need to be updated in the same way that you keep your wardrobe current by adding new items of clothing here and there and blending them with your old favorites. Transforming the look of your home can be as simple as rearranging your furniture and changing the cushion covers and afghans adorning your sofa, chairs or bed.

When it comes to knitting for your home, my advice is to splurge on big showcase pieces like afghans and cushion covers (because with proper care and storage they can last long enough to be passed down to future generations), and use stash yarn for smaller items like cozies and doilies. In addition to adorning your own living space, all the home decor projects make lovely gifts. No matter what your budget, you will find something you can give to even the pickiest recipient. Knit a dishcloth and the *Chichi Tea Towel* for your Nana. Knit a one-of-a-kind *Memphis Baby Blanket* for a mother-to-be. Or go all out and knit a *Bauhaus Geometric Throw* as a wedding present for a dear friend. No matter what the item or the occasion, the recipient is sure to love owning an original, handknit work of art! Play around with these patterns, make them your own, and create beautiful pieces that reflect your own unique spirit. I look forward to seeing your creations!

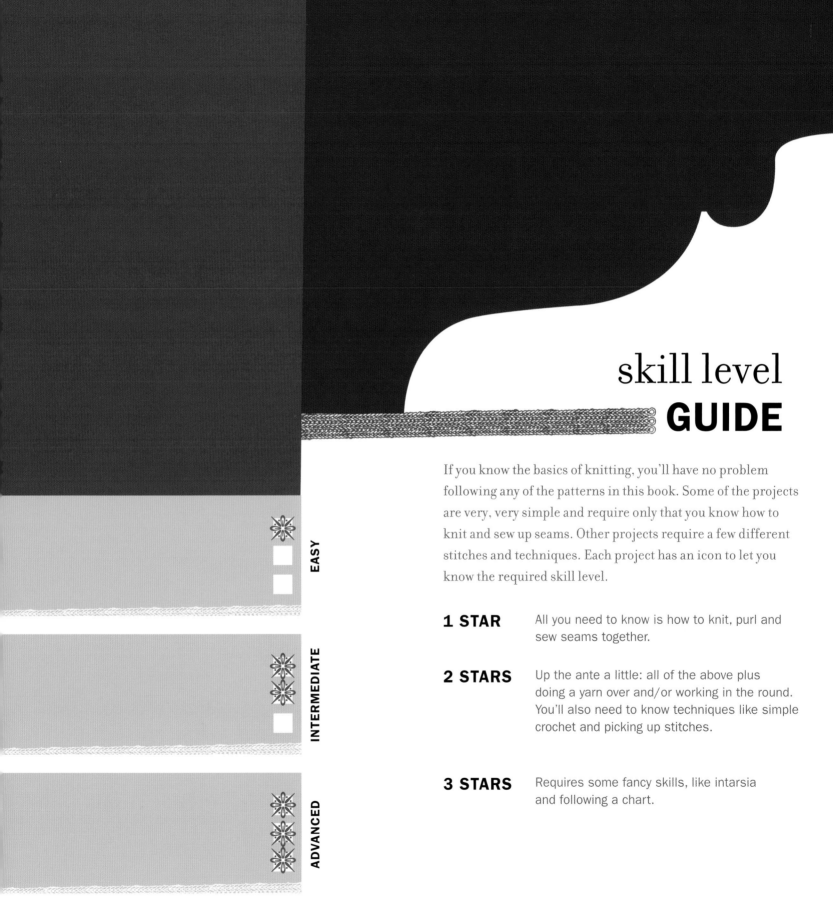

skill level
GUIDE

If you know the basics of knitting, you'll have no problem following any of the patterns in this book. Some of the projects are very, very simple and require only that you know how to knit and sew up seams. Other projects require a few different stitches and techniques. Each project has an icon to let you know the required skill level.

1 STAR All you need to know is how to knit, purl and sew seams together.

2 STARS Up the ante a little: all of the above plus doing a yarn over and/or working in the round. You'll also need to know techniques like simple crochet and picking up stitches.

3 STARS Requires some fancy skills, like intarsia and following a chart.

EASY

INTERMEDIATE

ADVANCED

CLOTHS + COZIES

Everyone who knows me or reads my blog knows I am crazy for cozies and cute little handknit cloths. I love the kitschiness of dressing up everyday objects like my beloved French press (see the *Oo La La French Press Cozy*). And I enjoy the look of wonder and delight on a friend's face when I present her with a gift covered in a lovely cozy (see the *Tune-Up CD Cozy*). For me, it honors the work of my daily chores to perform them with beautiful, handknit dishcloths and tea towels. "Serious" knitters often deem these projects silly. If a project isn't terribly complicated or obviously useful, they fail to find it worthwhile. But I get tremendous joy from whipping up a sweet little project. It gives me pleasure to lovingly attend to each detail with the same care and attention that I would bestow upon a larger project. Cuteness is not a crime! These cloths and cozies are quick knits meant to bring joy to your knitting and a knowing smile to your face.

Need a break from your "serious" knitting projects?
Why not try your hand at knitting a cozy? Cozies are great because they are frivolous, fabulous and totally fun! A little while ago I found myself in need of a quick and inexpensive birthday gift for a pal. I burned a mixed CD of some of my favorite songs, but somehow that just didn't seem like enough. I wanted to personalize my gift in some way. Thus, the CD cozy was born. Handmade gifts are great, but handmade wrapping is the icing on the cake! This cute cozy can be used for gift-giving or for carrying a favorite CD around in your tote bag.

tune-up
{ CD COZY }

CONSTRUCTION NOTES

This stash-busting project can be knit with leftover bits of sock yarn! When joining a new yarn, overlap it with the previous yarn and knit with both yarns together for three or four stitches. Then cut the first yarn, leaving a 1" (3cm) tail, and continue knitting with the new yarn.

MEASUREMENTS
5½" x 5" (14cm x 13cm)

YARN
150 yds (137m) fingering or sport-weight yarn

a few yards (meters) of yarn in a contrasting color for edging

NEEDLES + NOTIONS
size US 3 (3.25mm) needles

size D (3.25mm) crochet hook

If necessary, change needle size to obtain correct gauge.

two ½" (1cm) buttons

tapestry needle

sewing needle and thread

GAUGE
26 sts and 51 rows = 4" (10cm) in garter st on size 3 (3.25mm) needles

CD COZY
Cast on 36 sts. Work in garter st for 13¾" (35cm).

BUTTONHOLE ROW: K6, yo, k2tog, work to last 8 sts, k2tog, yo, knit to end.

Knit 7 rows. Bind off.

FINISHING
With contrast color yarn, work 1 row of slip st crochet along the edge of the flap (see the Glossary for instructions on working in slip st crochet).

Fold up the bottom of the Cozy to approx 5¼" (13cm). Sew the side seams with a tapestry needle and scrap yarn. Use a sewing needle and thread to sew on buttons, aligning them with the buttonholes.

"A Wine Bottle Sweater? Whatever for?" you exclaim. To which I happily reply, "Because it's cute, it's fun, and if you are at all like me you probably have a lot of yarn and a lot of wine bottles lying about." And even if you aren't like me and you don't have too much yarn and too many wine bottles, it is still a cool cozy to accompany a bottle of wine you are taking to a dinner party. Or if you just love kitschy cozies, you can bust out your stash bin, make a few, and use them to decorate a bar or to create a tabletop centerpiece.

chilled
{ WINE BOTTLE SWEATER }

CONSTRUCTION NOTES

The *Wine Bottle Sweater* is knit in the round using double-pointed needles. Worked from the bottom up, simple decreases shape the form-fitting "neck."

MEASUREMENTS
approx 10¼" (26cm) tall

YARN
1 skein Filatura Di Crosa 127 Print (100% wool, 93 yds [85m] per 50g)
   color #14 off-white with tans and browns

Or substitute 60 yds (55m) of any worsted weight yarn.

NEEDLES
size US 8 (5mm) DPNs

If necessary, change needle size to obtain correct gauge.

GAUGE
16 sts and 28 rows = 4" (10cm)

WINE BOTTLE SWEATER

Cast on 36 sts. Divide sts evenly over DPNs. Join for working in the rnd, taking care not to twist sts.

Work in k2, p2 rib for 8 rnds.

Change to St st, inc 2 sts evenly spaced over next rnd—38 sts.

Work even until piece measures 8" (20cm), or desired body length from cast-on edge.

DECREASE FOR TOP

RND 1: * K4, k2tog; rep from * to last 2 sts, k2—32 sts.

RNDS 2–3: Knit.

RND 4: * K2, k2tog; rep from * to end of rnd—24 sts.

RNDS 5–6: Knit.

RND 7: * K2, k2tog; rep from * to end of rnd—18 sts.

RNDS 8–9: Knit.

RND 10: K7, k2tog twice—16 sts.

Work in k2, p2 rib for 8 rnds. Bind off.

When I was drawing up the project list for YarnPlay at Home, I asked my blog readers what kind of cozy pattern they would most like to see in a book, and the majority of those who responded suggested a French press cozy. And voilá, the *Oo La La French Press Cozy* was born! I love the idea of adorning objects that I use on a daily basis. Whether your mission is to cleverly conceal your French press or to bring a shot of color to your kitchen countertop, this cozy is super-cute and quick to knit.

oo la la
{ FRENCH PRESS COZY }

CONSTRUCTION NOTES

The body of the *French Press Cozy* is knit as a flat piece of fabric. After seaming and transferring the stitches to double-pointed needles, you will work the top portion in the round.

MEASUREMENTS
10½" (27cm) high x
12" (30cm) around

YARN
1 skein of Scout's Swag Super-wash Worsted (100% merino wool, 175 yds [160m])
    color Blue in Green

Or substitute 150 yds (137m) of any worsted weight yarn.

NEEDLES + NOTIONS
size US 8 (5mm) straight needles

size US 8 (5mm) DPNs

If necessary, change needle size to obtain correct gauge.

tapestry needle

GAUGE
18 sts and 28 rows = 4" (10cm) in patt

FRENCH PRESS COZY

With straight needles, CO 54 sts.

BEGIN PATTERN

ROW 1: K1, kfb in each st to last st, k1.

ROW 2: K1, * k2tog, p2tog; rep from * to last st, k1.

Rep Rows 1–2 until piece measures 6¾" (17cm), ending with Row 2.

Knit 8 rows.

Leaving yarn attached, place sts on a piece of waste yarn.

Leaving an open space for the handle, sew the side seam above and below the handle.

Place sts on DPNs. Remove waste yarn.

Knit 2 rnds.

TOP DECREASES

RND 1: * K7, k2tog; rep from * to end of rnd—48 sts.

RNDS 2–3: Knit.

RND 4: * K6, k2tog; rep from* to end of rnd—42 sts.

RND 5: Knit.

RND 6: * K5, k2tog; rep from * to end of rnd—36 sts.

RND 7: Knit.

RND 8: * K4, k2tog; rep from * to end of rnd—30 sts.

RND 9: Knit.

RND 10: * K3, k2tog; rep from * to end of rnd—24 sts.

RND 11: Knit.

RND 12: * K2, k2tog; rep from * to end of rnd—18 sts.

RND 13: Knit.

RND 14: * K1, k2tog; rep from * to end of rnd—12 sts.

Knit 5 rnds.

FINAL RND: K2tog around—6 sts.

Cut yarn and pull through rem sts. Finish off. Weave in ends.

tic tac
{ DISHCLOTH }

A dishcloth is the perfect project to knit on the go!
Knit a few rows on your subway ride to work or while you're
waiting for an appointment. Inexpensive and quick to knit, a
dishcloth is the perfect little project on which to perfect your
knitting skills. You may want to keep a few extra on hand,
because these sweet dishcloths make great gifts.

CONSTRUCTION NOTES

The Tic Tac pattern is perfect for beginners. It's a simple four-row repeating pattern that differs
only slightly from row to row. Try the *Serpentine Dishcloth* when you are ready for more of a
challenge.

MEASUREMENTS
11" x 11" (28cm x 28cm)

YARN
1 skein Lion Brand Lion Cotton (100%
cotton, 189 yds [170m] per 113g)
   color #257 Cornmeal

Or substitute 140 yds (128m) of any wor-
sted weight cotton.

NEEDLES
size US 6 (4mm) needles

If necessary, change needle size
to obtain correct gauge.

GAUGE
16 sts and 24 rows = 4" (10cm)
in patt

DISHCLOTH
CO 42 sts.

Knit 2 rows.

BEGIN PATTERN

ROW 1: K3, p1, * k1, p1; rep from *
to last 2 sts, k2.

ROW 2: K2, * p1, k1; rep from *
to last 2 sts, k2.

ROW 3: K2, * p1, k1; rep from *
to last 2 sts, k2.

ROW 4: K3, p1, * k1, p1; rep from *
to last 2 sts, k2.

Rep Rows 1–4 until piece
measures approx 10½" (27cm),
ending with Row 4.

Knit 2 rows. Bind off.
Weave in ends.

serpentine
{ DISHCLOTH }

This lovely dishcloth is perfect for a new knitter who is up for a challenge, but who isn't ready to invest a lot of time or a load of cash into her next project. And more experienced knitters can whip this up in no time!

CONSTRUCTION NOTES

The yarn overs and decreases in this pattern create pretty peek-a-boo eyelets, and the staggered knits and purls produce dimensional ribs.

MEASUREMENTS
11" x 11" (28cm x 28cm)

YARN
1 skein of Lion Brand Lion Cotton
(100% cotton, 236 yds [212m]
per 113g)
>color #157 Sunflower

*Or substitute 140 yds (128m)
of any worsted weight cotton yarn.*

NEEDLES
size US 6 (4mm) needles

*If necessary, change needle size
to obtain correct gauge.*

GAUGE
16 sts and 24 rows = 4" (10cm)
in St st

DISHCLOTH
CO 42 sts.

Knit 2 rows.

BEGIN PATTERN

ROW 1 (RS): K2, p2, * yo, k1, yo, p2;
rep from * to last 2 sts, k2.

ROW 2 (WS): K4, * p3, k2; rep from *
to last 2 sts, k2.

ROW 3: K2, p2, * k3, p2; rep from *
to last 2 sts, k2.

ROW 4: K4, * p3tog, k2; rep from *
to last 2 sts, k2.

Rep Rows 1–4 until piece measures
approx 10½" (27cm), ending with
Row 4.

Knit 2 rows. Bind off.
Weave in ends.

chichi
{ TEA TOWEL }

In the case of this bright dish towel, "Chichi" is short for cheap and cheerful. If you are pressed for money or time, this is the perfect project! It's portable enough to take with you when you travel, and it's simple enough to serve as TV knitting. Paired with a handknit dishcloth, it makes a great gift. You could also pair this towel with a washcloth-sized version and use it in a guest bathroom.

CONSTRUCTION NOTES

The *Chichi Tea Towel* is easy to knit, but the optional crochet border raises the skill level to 2 stars.

MEASUREMENTS
16" x 21" (41cm x 53cm)

YARN
1 skein Lion Brand Lion Cotton (100% cotton, 236 yds [212m] per 113g)
    color #108 Morning Glory Blue

several yards (meters) of yarn in a contrasting color for edging

Or substitute 236 yds (212m) of any worsted weight cotton yarn.

NEEDLES + HOOKS
size US 7 (4.5mm) needles

If necessary, change needle size to obtain correct gauge.

size G (4.25mm) crochet hook

GAUGE
16 sts and 24 rows = 4" (10cm) in patt on size US 7 (4.5mm) needles

TEA TOWEL
Cast on 63 sts. Knit 2 rows.

BEGIN PATTERN

ROW 1: K10, p3, (k7, p3) 4 times, k10.

ROW 2: K3, (p7, k3) 6 times.

Rep Rows 1–2 until piece measures 20½" (52cm) from cast-on edge, ending with Row 2.

Knit 2 rows. Bind off.

FINISHING
With contrast color yarn, work 1 rnd of single crochet around edges. (See the Glossary for instructions on working a single crochet border.)

BED, BATH
+ BABY

On any given Saturday, you might find me strolling around a museum or gallery. I enjoy viewing artists' unique interpretations of universal themes and elements, and I am always drawn to the repetition of various designs throughout the ages. They make an impression upon my consciousness, and consequently, they sometimes emerge in my own work. From the bold, outsider art vibe of the Gee's Bend quilts and the austerity of the Bauhaus movement to the vivacious designs of the late 1960s, great works and movements serve as influence and inspiration for the designs in this chapter. For example, the *Memphis Baby Blanket* pays homage to one of my favorite Gee's Bend artists. And the *Barcelona Four-Square Afghan* is my tribute to a popular design motif from the 1960s and 1970s. You can follow the patterns as they are written or play around and create a design or color arrangement that speaks to your spirit.

There is nothing that I treasure more than a good night's sleep. Creating a haven of comfort and beauty in my bedroom is essential to my well-being. When I designed the Kathmandu sham and matching pillow, I envisioned a pampered princess reclining on a lofty bed covered with sumptuous linens and big, fluffy pillows. This enchanting set will bring a feeling of luxury to even the most boring bedroom. Sweet dreams!

kathmandu set
{ BED SHAM + THROW PILLOW }

CONSTRUCTION NOTES

One skein of Lorna's Laces Heaven makes both the sham and the smaller pillow. Unexpected bumps of knit-and-purl in the middle of smooth Stockinette stitch create surprising texture in these luxurious pillow covers.

BED SHAM

MEASUREMENTS

25" x 19" (64cm x 48cm)

YARN

1 skein Lorna's Laces Heaven (mohair/nylon blend, 975 yds [891m] per 198g)
    color Black Purl

1 skein makes the Bed Sham *and the* Throw Pillow.

NEEDLES + NOTIONS

29" to 32" (74cm to 81cm) size US 8 (5mm) circular needles

If necessary, change needle size to obtain correct gauge.

four 1" (3cm) buttons

tapestry needle

safety pins

sewing needle and thread

GAUGE

16 sts and 26 rows = 4" (10cm) in St st

Gauge is the same for the Bed Sham *and the* Throw Pillow.

THROW PILLOW

MEASUREMENTS

14" x 17" (36cm x 43cm)

NEEDLES + NOTIONS

size US 8 (5mm) circular needles

If necessary, change needle size to obtain correct gauge.

three 1" (3cm) buttons

tapestry needle

safety pins

sewing needle and thread

See Bed Sham *for yarn and gauge information.*

BED SHAM

FRONT

Cast on 75 sts.

Knit 4 rows.

BEGIN PATTERN

ROW A (RS): Knit.

ROW B (WS): K3, purl to last 3 sts, k3.

Rep Rows A–B until piece measures 3" (8cm), ending with Row B.

ROW C (RS): K14, p1, * k1, p1; rep from * to last 14 sts, k14.

ROW D (WS): K3, p12, * k1, p1; rep from * to last 14 sts, p11, k3.

Rep Rows C–D 6 times.

ROW E (RS): K14, p1, (k1, p1) 4 times, k29, p1, (k1, p1) 4 times, k14.

ROW F (WS): K3, p12, (k1, p1) 4 times, p30, (k1, p1) 4 times, p11, k3.

Rep Rows E–F until piece measures 20" (51cm) from cast-on edge, ending with Row F.

Rep Rows C–D 7 times.

Rep Rows A–B until piece measures 24½" (62cm) from cast-on edge, ending with Row B.

Knit 4 rows. Place a safety pin at each end of last row to mark start of Flap.

FLAP

Rep Rows A–B until piece measures 32" (81cm) from cast-on edge, ending with Row B.

BUTTONHOLE ROW (RS): K7, (k2tog, yo twice, k2tog, k15) 3 times, k2tog, yo twice, k2tog, k7.

NEXT ROW: K3, purl to last 3 sts, k3.

NEXT ROW: K3, * p1, k1; rep from * to last 4 sts, p1, k3.

Rep last row 5 times.

Bind off.

BACK

Cast on 75 sts. Knit 4 rows.

BEGIN PATTERN

ROW A (RS): Knit.

ROW B (WS): K3, purl to last 3 sts, k3.

Rep Rows A–B until piece measures 24½" (62cm), ending with Row 2.

Knit 4 rows. Bind off.

FINISHING

Seam the bottom and sides of the Front and Back pieces using a tapestry needle and scrap yarn. Use a sewing needle and thread to sew on buttons, aligning them with the buttonholes. Weave in ends.

THROW PILLOW

The *Throw Pillow* is knit in one piece beginning at the top of the Back.

Cast on 55 sts.

Knit 4 rows.

BEGIN PATTERN

ROW A (RS): Knit.

ROW B (WS): K3, purl to last 3 sts, k3.

Rep Rows A–B until piece measures 13½" (34cm), ending with Row B.

Knit 4 rows, then place a safety pin at beg and end of row to mark bottom edge of Pillow.

Knit 4 rows.

Rep Rows A–B until piece measures 18" (46cm), ending with Row B.

ROW C (RS): K15, * p1, k1; rep from * to last 16 sts, p1, k15.

ROW D (WS): K3, p13, * k1, p1; rep from * to last 15 sts, p12, k3.

Rep Rows C–D until piece measures 24" (61cm), ending with Row D.

Rep Rows A–B until piece measures 27½" (70cm), ending with Row B.

Knit 4 rows, then place a safety pin at beg and end of row to mark top of Pillow.

FLAP

Rep Rows A–B until piece measures 32" (81cm), ending with Row B.

BUTTONHOLE ROW (RS): K12, k2tog, yo twice, k2tog, k23, k2tog, yo twice, k2tog, k12.

NEXT ROW: K3, purl to last 3 sts, k3.

NEXT ROW: K3, * p1, k1; rep from * to last 4 sts, p1, k3.

Rep last row 5 times.

Bind off.

FINISHING
Use a tapestry needle and scrap yarn to sew the side seams as marked by the safety pins. Use a sewing needle and thread to sew on buttons to align with the buttonholes. Weave in ends.

bauhaus
{ GEOMETRIC THROW }

When I designed this blanket, I was thinking of the Bauhaus art movement with its stern and unadorned style. My aim was to create a piece that is both sleek and clean, as well as moody and sumptuous. This inviting throw adds warmth to an ultra-modern decor without causing distraction, giving the *Bauhaus Geometric Throw* a twenty-first-century look.

CONSTRUCTION NOTES

The squares are arranged so that one color shows horizontal garter ridges and the other vertical ridges.

MEASUREMENTS
52" x 52" (132cm x 132cm)

Throw is comprised of 4 26" x 26" (66cm x 66cm) squares.

YARN
1 skein Lorna's Laces Heaven (mohair/nylon blend, 975 yds [891m] per 198g) in each of the foll colors:
> *color Pewter (A)*
> *color Blackberry (B)*

Or substitute 975 yds (891m) of any worsted weight mohair yarn for each color.

NEEDLES + NOTIONS
29" to 32" (74cm to 80cm) size US 10 (6mm) circular needle

If necessary, change needle size to obtain correct gauge.

tapestry needle

GAUGE
14 sts and 28 rows = 4" (10cm) in garter st

GEOMETRIC THROW

Cast on 92 sts. Work in garter st until square measures 26" (66cm).

Bind off.

Knit 2 squares with Color A and 2 squares with Color B.

FINISHING

Sew squares together with mattress stitch, turning one pair of colors so that the garter ridges run vertically. (See the Glossary for illustrated instructions on working in mattress stitch.)

The Potluck Patchwork Pillow *is a stash-busting project that combines different colors and textures to create a unique take on a traditional design.* I chose one of my favorite colors, in merino wool, to use as the main color. Next, for a different texture I added a silk/mohair blend as one of two contrast colors. I purposely chose a color that was only partly complementary to the main color. I find that working with colors that are slightly off brings a bit of depth to the project at hand. For the second contrast color I double-stranded leftover bits of sport-weight yarn. I chose the colors randomly from my stash, creating a "potluck" effect. This is a great way to use up leftover bits of sock yarn!

potluck
{ PATCHWORK PILLOW }

CONSTRUCTION NOTES

Each of the five vertical strips is made of five squares and is knit in one piece, starting from the bottom. The button bands are double-sided, separated by a turning ridge. On the front you will pick up stitches along the top border of the five strips to create the button band. The back is knit in one piece starting with the bottom and ending with the button band at the top.

MEASUREMENTS
14" x 14" (36cm x 36cm)

YARN
1 skein Lorna's Laces Shepherd Worsted (100% superwash wool, 225 yds [206m] per 113g)
> color Pink Blossom (MC)

Or substitute 225 yds (206m) of any worsted weight yarn.

1 skein Rowan Kidsilk Haze (mohair/silk blend, 227 yds [207m] per 25g), working with 2 strands held tog
> color 632 Hurricane (CC1)

Or substitute 100 yds (91m) of a single strand of any lightweight yarn.

approx 250 yds (228m) of fingering/sport weight scrap yarn, working with 2 strands held tog
> variegated scrap yarns (CC2)

Or substitute 120 yds (110m) of a single strand of any worsted weight yarn.

NEEDLES + NOTIONS
size US 8 (5mm) needles

If necessary, change needle size to obtain correct gauge.

five ⅞" (2cm) buttons

one 14" x 14" (36cm x 36cm) pillow insert

tapestry needle

sewing needle and thread

GAUGE
19 sts and 28 rows = 4" (10cm) in St st with MC

59

PATCHWORK PILLOW

FRONT

The Front of the Pillow is knit in 5 separate vertical strips, knit from the bottom up. For each strip, cast on 14 sts and work in St st in the color indicated by the chart until the square measures 2¾" (7cm) long, ending with a WS row.

Change colors and rep until you have completed 5 squares. Bind off. Keep 1 st at beg and end of every row in garter st, and work first 2 and last 2 rows of each strip in garter st.

Using mattress stitch, seam strips together as indicated by the chart. (See the Glossary for instructions on working in mattress stitch.)

BUTTON BAND

With MC, pick up and knit 66 sts across top edge of Front. (See the Glossary for instructions on picking up sts.)

Work 3 rows in St st, beg with a purl row.

BUTTONHOLE ROW (RS): K5, (yo, k2tog, k12) twice, (k2tog, yo, k12) twice, k2tog, yo, k5.

Beg with a purl row, cont in St st for 4 rows.

TURNING RIDGE

Knit next row (WS) for Turning Ridge. Cont in St st, beg with a knit row, for 4 rows.

NEXT ROW: Rep Buttonhole Row.

Beg with a purl row, cont in St st for 3 rows. Bind off.

BACK

With MC, cast on 66 sts.

Knit 2 rows.

ROW 1: Knit.

ROW 2: K3, purl to last 3 sts, k3.

Rep Rows 1–2 until piece measures 13¾" (35cm).

Knit 2 rows.

BUTTON BAND

Change to CC2. Beg with a knit row, work 9 rows of St st.

TURNING RIDGE

Knit next row (WS) for Turning Ridge. Cont in St st, beg with a knit row, for 8 rows.

Bind off.

FINISHING

Seam the Back and Front of the Pillow tog.

Fold each Button Band to WS on Turning Ridge. With yarn threaded on a tapestry needle, slip stitch the Button Band in place.

Attach the buttons opposite buttonholes with a sewing needle and thread. Weave in any ends.

KEY

MC Lorna's Laces
Shepherd Worsted
Pink Blossom

CC1 Rowan Kidsilk Haze
632 Hurricane
2 strands held tog

CC2 Fingering/Sport Weight
variegated scrap yarns
2 strands held tog

Potluck Patchwork Pillow *Diagram*

MC	CC2	MC	CC2	MC
CC2	CC1	CC2	CC1	CC2
CC1	CC2	MC	CC2	CC1
CC2	CC1	CC2	CC1	CC2
MC	CC2	MC	CC2	MC

This pattern of interlocking squares is often seen in designs from the late 1960s and early 1970s. I have seen it on carpets, curtains and fabric. Sometimes it looks terribly tacky, and at other times it looks super sophisticated. I love designs that give you pause and really make you think about whether or not they appeal to you. There are so many ways you can play around with this pattern. You could use the same main color for all of the squares or use several colors instead of just one contrast color. Feel free to interpret this design and make it your own!

barcelona
{ FOUR-SQUARE AFGHAN }

CONSTRUCTION NOTES

This afghan is composed of sixteen individually knit squares. Knit them as indicated by the charts and arrange accordingly. Intarsia charts are read from right to left on odd-numbered rows, and from left to right on even-numbered rows. Usually all the stitches on odd-numbered rows are knit, and those on even-numbered rows are purled. However, for this design you will knit the first two and last two stitches on every row. Make sure to pay close attention to the pattern, as it calls for knitting some rows to create a garter stitch border.

MEASUREMENTS
48" x 57" (122cm x 145cm)

YARN
3 skeins Rowan Scottish Tweed Chunky (100% wool, 109 yds [100m] per 100g) in each of the following colors:

    color #024 Porridge
    color #023 Midnight
    color #017 Lobster
    color #007 Lewis Gray
    color #026 Rose

Or substitute 327 yds (299m) of any chunky-weight wool for each color listed above.

NEEDLES + NOTIONS
size US 11 (8mm) needles

If necessary, change needle size to obtain correct gauge.

tapestry needle

GAUGE
12 sts and 18 rows = 4" (10cm) in St st

FOUR-SQUARE AFGHAN

Each large square is composed of 4 smaller squares. For each smaller square, cast on 36 sts with the color indicated and foll the chart for that particular square. Knit the first and last 2 sts of each row, plus knit every st of the foll rows: 1, 2, 63 and 64, to make a garter st border.

FINISHING

Block each square before seaming. Seam squares tog with mattress stitch according to the Construction Diagram. (See the Glossary for instructions on working in mattress stitch.) Weave in any ends.

KEY

Square A:	MC = Porridge
	CC1 = Midnight
	CC2 = Lobster
Square B:	MC = Rose
	CC1 = Midnight
	CC2 = Porridge
Square C:	MC = Lewis Gray
	CC1 = Midnight
	CC2 = Rose
Square D:	MC = Lobster
	CC1 = Midnight
	CC2 = Lewis Gray

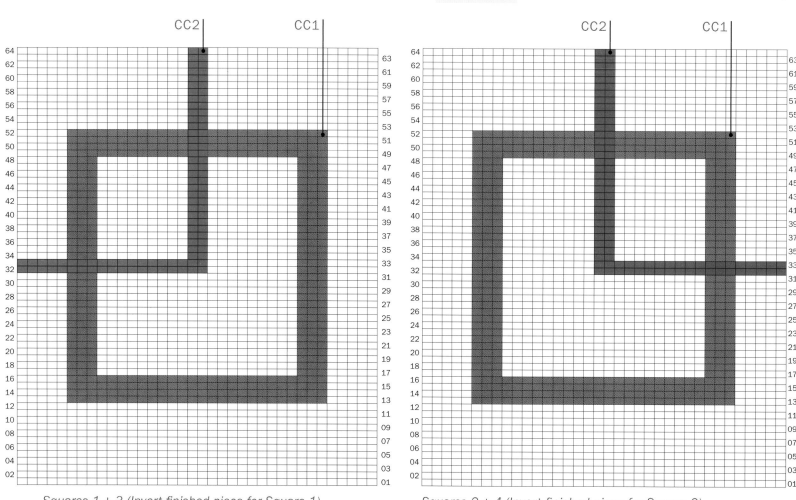

CC2   CC1

CC2   CC1

Squares 1 + 3 (Invert finished piece for Square 1)

Squares 2 + 4 (Invert finished piece for Square 2)

KEY

☐ = MC

▨ = CC1

▨ = CC2

Knit on odd-numbered rows; purl on even-numbered rows.

Note the foll exceptions: Knit the first and last 2 sts on every row.

Rows 1, 2, 63, 64 knit every st.

Four-Square Afghan *Construction Diagram*

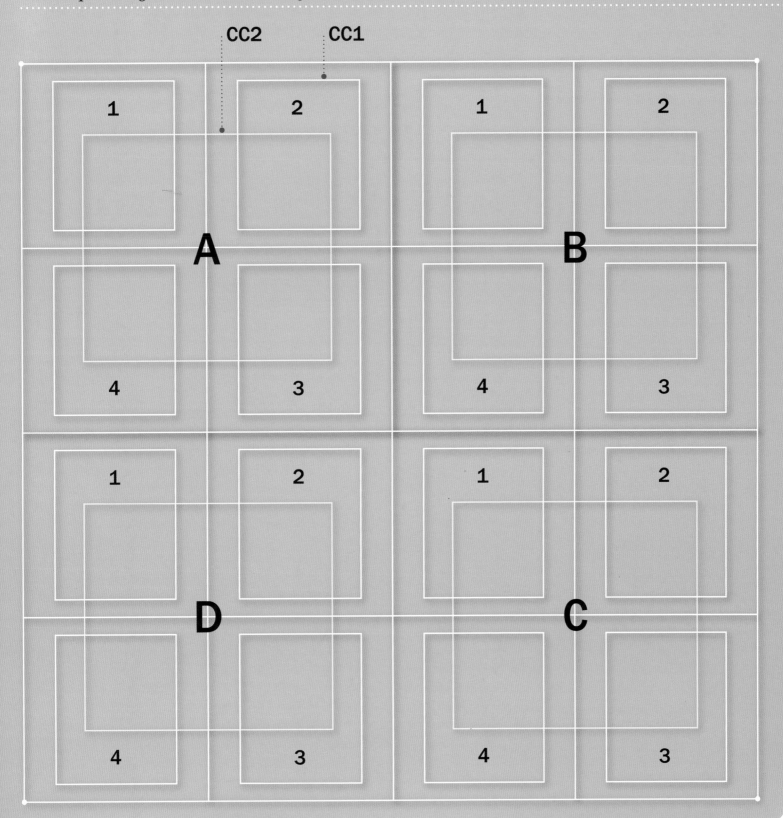

everyday

{ BATH MAT }

I have yet to meet a knitter who doesn't have a family member or close friend whom they really want to knit for, but who complains that all sweaters are scratchy and that just the thought of wearing handknit socks makes her feet sweat! Everyone can use an *Everyday Bath Mat.* Both novices and seasoned knitters alike will find this easy and elegant project fun to knit.

CONSTRUCTION NOTES

You will be knitting with two strands of yarn held together throughout this simple striped seed stitch pattern.

MEASUREMENTS
22" x 32" (56cm x 81cm)

YARN
2 skeins Lion Brand Lion Cotton (100% cotton, 236 yds [212m] per 113g)
   color # 98 Natural

Or substitute 472 yds (431m) of any worsted weight cotton yarn.

NEEDLES
29" to 32" (74cm to 81cm) size US 10½ (6.5mm) circular needle

If necessary, change needle size to obtain correct gauge.

GAUGE
Working with 2 strands held tog, 14 sts and 22 rows = 4" (10cm) in patt

BATH MAT
Using 2 strands of yarn held tog, cast on 73 sts. Knit 2 rows.

BEGIN PATTERN

ROW 1 (RS): K6, * (k1, p1) 3 times, k5; rep from * to last st, k1.

ROW 2 (WS): K1, * p5, (p1, k1) 3 times; rep from * to last 6 sts, p5, k1.

Rep Rows 1–2 until piece measures approx 31½" (80cm), ending with Row 1.

Knit 2 rows. Bind off. Weave in any ends.

memphis
{ BABY BLANKET }

My inspiration for this blanket was a quilt created by the Gee's Bend artist, Polly Bennett. My initial impulse was to create a literal, knitted interpretation of her quilt, but then, almost immediately, I became bored with that idea. I set my sketches aside for a few days, and when I picked them up again I felt inspired to create a design that paid homage to Ms. Bennett's work while reflecting my own spirit and aesthetic. Similarly, I hope that you will take inspiration from my design and use it as a springboard to find a pattern that speaks to you.

CONSTRUCTION NOTES

Knit squares in the sequence indicated if you want to keep color continuity from one square to the next. Or not! My design is merely a suggestion. Play around with the arrangement of the squares and see what emerges.

MEASUREMENTS
30" x 30" (76cm x 76cm)

YARN
2 skeins Debbie Bliss Merino Aran (100% merino wool, 85 yds [77m] per 50g) in each of the foll colors:
> color #208 lavender (A)
> color #702 grape (B)

Or substitute 172 yds (157m) of any worsted weight yarn for each color.

2 skeins of Noro Kureyon (100% wool, 110 yds [100m] per 50g) in each of the foll colors:
> color #52 blue/violet/chartreuse (C)
> color #147 blues/greens (D)
> color #166 green/teal/pink/purple (E)

Or substitute 220 yds (201m) of any worsted weight yarn for each color.

NEEDLES + NOTIONS
size US 8 (5mm) needles

If necessary, change needle size to obtain correct gauge.

tapestry needle

GAUGE
18 sts and 30 rows = 4" (10cm) in garter st

BABY BLANKET

SQUARE 1
With E, cast on 40 sts. Work in garter st for 3" (8cm). Change to A, work in garter st for 3" (8cm). Change to C, work in garter st for 3" (8cm). Bind off.

SQUARE 2
With A, cast on 40 sts. Work in garter st for 3" (8cm). Change to C, work in garter st for 3" (8cm). Change to B, work in garter st for 3" (8cm). Bind off.

SQUARE 3
With E, cast on 40 sts. Work in garter st for 3" (8cm). Change to B, work in garter st for 3" (8cm). Change to D, work in garter st for 3" (8cm). Bind off.

SQUARE 4
With D, cast on 40 sts. Work in garter st for 3" (8cm). Change to A, work in garter st for 3" (8cm). Change to C, work in garter st for 3" (8cm). Bind off.

SQUARE 5
With C, cast on 40 sts. Work in garter st for 3" (8cm). Change to B, work in garter st for 3" (8cm). Change to E, work in garter st for 3" (8cm). Bind off.

SQUARE 6
With B, cast on 40 sts. Work in garter st for 3" (8cm). Change to C, work in garter st for 3" (8cm). Change to A, work in garter st for 3" (8cm). Bind off.

SQUARE 7
With D, cast on 40 sts. Work in garter st for 3" (8cm). Change to A, work in garter st for 3" (8cm). Change to E, work in garter st for 3" (8cm). Bind off.

SQUARE 8
With D, cast on 40 sts. Work in garter st for 3" (8cm). Change to B, work in garter st for 3" (8cm). Change to C, work in garter st for 3" (8cm). Bind off.

SQUARE 9
With A, cast on 40 sts. Work in garter st for 3" (8cm). Change to E, work in garter st for 3" (8cm). Change to B, work in garter st for 3" (8cm). Bind off.

FINISHING
Block squares to 9¼" x 9¼" (23cm x 23cm). Seam squares tog as indicated.

BORDER
With RS facing and using D, pick up and knit 123 sts along side I. (See the Glossary for instructions on picking up sts.) Work in seed st for 9 rows, inc 1 st at each end of every other row, working inc into the patt. (See the Glossary for instructions on working in seed st.) Bind off.

With RS facing and using C, pick up and knit 123 sts along side II. Work in seed st for 9 rows, inc 1 st at each end of every other row, working inc into the patt. Bind off.

With RS facing and using D, pick up and knit 123 sts along side III. Work in seed st for 9 rows, inc 1 st at each end of every other row, working inc into the patt. Bind off.

With RS facing and using E, pick up and knit 123 sts along side IV. Work in seed st for 9 rows, inc 1 st at each end of every other row, working inc into the patt. Bind off.

Seam corners of border. Weave in ends.

KEY

A	Debbie Bliss *merino aran 208 lavender*
B	Debbie Bliss *merino aran 702 grape*
C	Kureyon 52
D	Kureyon 147
E	Kureyon 166

Memphis Baby Blanket *Construction Diagram*

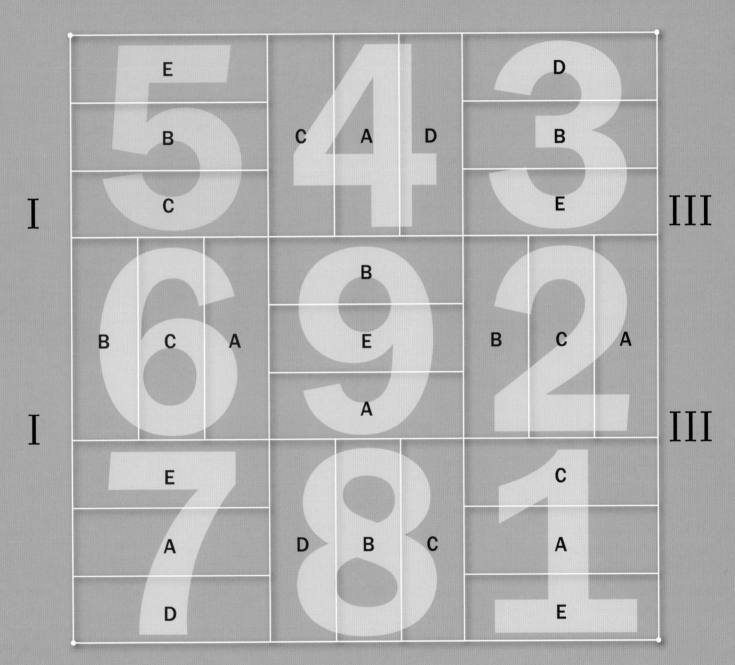

printemps
{ RECEIVING BLANKET }

It is no secret that I love color! However, every now and then I like a little texture, too. When combining both elements, it is usually best to keep things simple. Less is definitely more when working with a variegated color. A simple textured stitch allows the beauty of a hand-dyed yarn to speak for itself. The combination is pleasing to both the hand and the eye. A simple crocheted border gives definition and a polished finish to this sweet receiving blanket.

CONSTRUCTION NOTES
Experiment with the crocheted border. You may use more rounds, or fewer, until you find the look you like best.

MEASUREMENTS
approx 29" x 29" (74cm x 74cm)

YARN
7 skeins of Artyarns Supermerino (100% merino, 104 yds [95m] per 50g)
    color #sm105 variegated
        pink and green (MC)

Or substitute 728 yds (665m) of any aran/worsted weight wool yarn.

1 skein of Artyarns Supermerino
    color #sm214 rose (CC)

Or substitute 104 yds (95m) of any aran/worsted weight wool yarn.

NEEDLES + HOOKS
size US 9 (5.5mm) needles

If necessary, change needle size to obtain correct gauge.

size I (5.5mm) crochet hook

GAUGE
18 sts and 28 rows = 4" (10cm) in patt on size US 9 (5.5mm) needles

RECEIVING BLANKET

With MC, cast on 126 sts.

Knit 2 rows.

BEGIN PATTERN

ROW 1 (RS): Knit.

ROW 2 (WS): K2, * k1, p1; rep from * to last 2 sts, k2.

ROW 3: Knit.

ROW 4: K2, * p1, k1; rep from * to last 2 sts, k2.

Rep Rows 1–4 until piece measures approx 27½" (70cm), ending with Row 4.

Knit 2 rows. Bind off.

FINISHING

Block Blanket before adding crochet border.

With CC, work 1 rnd of slip st crochet, followed by 2 rnds of single crochet around the edges. (See the Glossary for instructions on working
in slip st and single crochet.)

HOUSE + HOME

WHEN SOMEONE MENTIONS KNITTING FOR THE HOME, AFGHANS AND CUSHION COVERS IMMEDIATELY COME TO MIND. To me, that's just the starting point for all the wonderful things you can create to add handmade touches to your home that are little pieces of your personality. My goal for this chapter is to provide you with quirky and interesting designs that will become a part of your everyday collection, as well as heirloom-worthy decoratives destined to be passed down to future generations. For the table, there are placemats, *Op Art Graphic Coasters* and even flirty napkin skirts. And the rug, *Celebration Table Runner*, doily and lacy mohair curtain in this chapter can be used to decorate any room in your home. I hope these projects will inspire you to create a more colorful way of living!

This afghan was influenced by the collage work of Dada husband-and-wife duo Hans Arp and Sophie Taeuber-Arp. Dada is an anti-art movement that began in Zurich, Switzerland, during World War I. Dadaists ignored prevailing aesthetics and cultural standards and sought to provoke the viewer to develop his or her own interpretation of the work presented. We have certainly entered a new age of knitting where the old rules need not apply. In the spirit of Dadaism, feel free to play around with the design and explore your own arrangement of colors.

dada
{ DENIM THROW }

CONSTRUCTION NOTES

This throw is knit in eleven separate strips, numbered from right to left. These yarns are meant to fade slightly with each wash, leaving a patina resembling your favorite pair of jeans. There is a slight shrinkage, so be sure to wash the yarn that you intend to use for seaming beforehand. If you would like to preserve the crisp look of your throw, opt for dry cleaning.

MEASUREMENTS
45" x 58" (114cm x 147cm)

YARN
6 skeins Rowan Denim (100% cotton 102 yds [93m] per 50g) in each of the foll colors:

    color #225 Nashville (A)
    color #229 Memphis (B)
    color #231 Tennessee (C)
    color #324 Ecru (D)

Or substitute 600 yds (548m) of dk weight cotton yarn for each color.

If necessary, change needle size to obtain correct gauge.

NEEDLES + NOTIONS
size US 6 (4mm) needles

If necessary, change needle size to obtain correct gauge.

tapestry needle

GAUGE
20 sts and 28 rows = 4" (10cm) in St st

DENIM THROW

STRIP 1

With C, cast on 16 sts.

Knit 4 rows.

BEGIN PATTERN

ROW 1 (RS): Knit.

ROW 2 (WS): K2, p10, k4.

Rep Rows 1–2 until piece measures 14½" (37cm), ending with a WS row.

Change to A and cont in est patt for 14½" (37cm), ending with a WS row.

Change to D and cont in est patt for 14½" (37cm), ending with a WS row.

Change to B and cont in est patt for 14¼" (36cm), ending with a WS row.

Knit 4 rows. Bind off.

STRIP 2

With A, cast on 16 sts.

Knit 4 rows.

BEGIN PATTERN

ROW 1 (RS): Knit.

ROW 2 (WS): K2, p12, k2.

Rep Rows 1–2 until piece measures 14½" (37cm), ending with a WS row.

Change to B and cont in est patt for 14½" (37cm), ending with a WS row.

Change to C and cont in est patt for 14½" (37cm), ending with a WS row.

Change to D and cont in est patt for 14¼" (36cm), ending with a WS row.

Knit 4 rows. Bind off.

STRIP 3

With D, cast on 32 sts.

Knit 4 rows.

BEGIN PATTERN

ROW 1 (RS): Knit.

ROW 2 (WS): K2, p28, k2.

Rep Rows 1–2 until piece measures 14½" (37cm), ending with a WS row.

Change to C and cont in est patt for 14½" (37cm), ending with a WS row.

Change to B and cont in est patt for 14½" (37cm), ending with a WS row.

Change to A and cont in est patt for 14¼" (36cm), ending with a WS row.

Knit 4 rows. Bind off.

STRIP 4

With B, cast on 16 sts.

Knit 4 rows.

BEGIN PATTERN

ROW 1 (RS): Knit.

ROW 2 (WS): K2, p12, k2.

Rep Rows 1–2 until piece measures 14½" (37cm), ending with a WS row.

Change to D and cont in est patt for 14½" (37cm), ending with a WS row.

Change to A and cont in est patt for 14½" (37cm), ending with a WS row.

Change to C and cont in est patt for 14¼" (36cm), ending with a WS row.

Knit 4 rows. Bind off.

STRIP 5

With A, cast on 16 sts.

Knit 4 rows.

BEGIN PATTERN

ROW 1 (RS): Knit.

ROW 2 (WS): K2, p12, k2.

Rep Rows 1–2 until piece measures 14½" (37cm), ending with a WS row.

Change to B and cont in est patt for 14½" (37cm), ending with a WS row.

Change to C and cont in est patt for 14½" (37cm), ending with a WS row.

Change to D and cont in est patt for 14½" (37cm), ending with a WS row.

Knit 4 rows. Bind off.

STRIP 6

With B, cast on 32 sts.

Knit 4 rows.

BEGIN PATTERN

ROW 1 (RS): Knit.

ROW 2 (WS): K2, p28, k2.

Rep Rows 1–2 until piece measures 14½" (37cm), ending with a WS row.

Change to D and cont in est patt for 14½" (37cm), ending with a WS row.

Change to A and cont in est patt for 14½" (37cm), ending with a WS row.

Change to C and cont in est patt for 14¼" (36cm), ending with a WS row.

Knit 4 rows. Bind off.

STRIP 7

With D, cast on 16 sts.

Knit 4 rows.

BEGIN PATTERN

ROW 1 (**RS**): Knit.

ROW 2 (**WS**): K2, p12, k2.

Rep Rows 1–2 until piece measures 14½" (37cm), ending with a WS row.

Change to C and cont in est patt for 14½" (37cm), ending with a WS row.

Change to B and cont in patt for 14½" (37cm), ending with a WS row.

Change to A and cont in patt for 14¼" (36cm), ending with a WS row.

Knit 4 rows. Bind off.

STRIP 8

With C, cast on 16 sts.

Knit 4 rows.

BEGIN PATTERN

ROW 1 (RS): Knit.

ROW 2 (WS): K2, p12, k2.

Rep Rows 1–2 until piece measures 14½" (37cm), ending with a WS row.

Change to A and cont in est patt for 14½" (37cm), ending with a WS row.

Change to D and cont in patt for 14½" (37cm), ending with a WS row.

Change to B and cont in patt for 14¼" (36cm), ending with a WS row.

Knit 4 rows. Bind off.

STRIP 9

With A, cast on 32 sts.

Knit 4 rows.

BEGIN PATTERN

ROW 1 (**RS**): Knit.

ROW 2 (**WS**): K2, p28, k2.

Rep Rows 1–2 until piece measures 14½" (37cm), ending with a WS row.

Change to B and cont in est patt for 14½" (37cm), ending with a WS row.

Change to C and cont in patt for 14½" (37cm), ending with a WS row.

Change to D and cont in patt for 14¼" (36cm), ending with a WS row.

Knit 4 rows. Bind off.

STRIP 10

With D, cast on 16 sts.

Knit 4 rows.

BEGIN PATTERN

ROW 1 (RS): Knit.

ROW 2 (WS): K2, p12, k2.

Rep Rows 1–2 until piece measures 14½" (37cm), ending with a WS row.

Change to C and cont in est patt for 14½" (37cm), ending with a WS row.

Change to B and cont in patt for 14½" (37cm), ending with a WS row.

Change to A and cont in patt for 14¼" (36cm), ending with a WS row.

Knit 4 rows. Bind off.

STRIP 11

With B, cast on 16 sts.

Knit 4 rows.

BEGIN PATTERN

ROW 1 (**RS**): Knit.

ROW 2 (**WS**): k4, p10, k2.

Rep Rows 1–2 until piece measures 14½" (37cm), ending with a WS row.

Change to D and cont in est patt for 14½" (37cm), ending with a WS row.

Change to A and cont in patt for 14½" (37cm), ending with a WS row.

Change to C and cont in patt for 14¼" (36cm), ending with a WS row.

Knit 4 rows. Bind off.

FINISHING

Seam strips together in order given, using mattress stitch. (See the Glossary for instructions on working in mattress stitch.) Weave in ends.

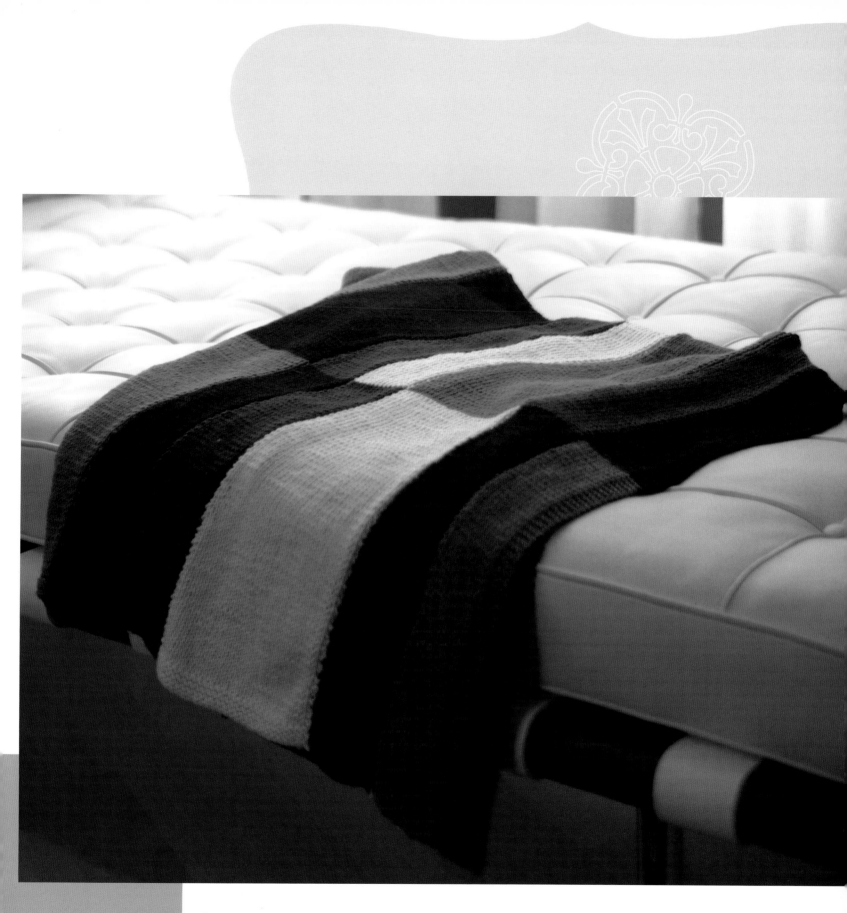

hudson
{ CUSHION COVER }

The Hudson Cushion Cover is sophisticated, and it has a slightly masculine feel, making it the perfect accent for a chair in a library or a man's study. Its textured pattern, combined with earthy blues and greens, gives it an organic quality that lends itself well to a room designed for comfort and contemplation. Its simple design works well with any color combination. Go camo with olive, charcoal and khaki, or give it a more tropical feel with turquoise, orange and lime. The possibilities are endless!

CONSTRUCTION NOTES

The back and top flap of this cushion cover are knit in one piece. The front is knit separately, then the two sides are seamed together. The pillow is worked in double moss stitch, a simple knit-and-purl pattern repeated over four rows that creates a very rich texture.

MEASUREMENTS
16" x 16" (41cm x 41cm)

YARN
1 skein Rowan Scottish Tweed Aran (100% wool, 186 yds [170m]) per 100g) in each of the foll colors:
> *color #002 Machair (A)*
> *color #031 Indigo (B)*
> *color #032 Lewis Blue (C)*
> *color #033 Lovat (D)*

Or substitute 186 yds (170m) of any worsted weight wool yarn for each color.

NEEDLES + NOTIONS
size US 8 (5mm) needles

If necessary, change needle size to obtain correct gauge.

four ¾" (19mm) buttons

one 14" x 14" (36cm x 36cm) pillow insert

safety pins

tapestry needle

GAUGE
17 sts and 28 rows = 4" (10cm) in St st

DOUBLE MOSS STITCH
Worked over a multiple of 4 sts.

ROW 1: * K2, p2; rep from * to end.

ROW 2: * K2, p2; rep from * to end.

ROW 3: * P2, k2; rep from * to end.

ROW 4: * P2, k2; rep from * to end.

Rep Rows 1–4.

CUSHION COVER

BACK

With D, cast on 48 sts.

Knit 2 rows.

Note: The patt beg on a WS row.

Change to A and work in double moss st until piece measures 5¼" (13cm), ending with Row 2 or 4.

Knit 1 row.

Change to B and knit 1 row. Cont in double moss st, beg with Row 1, until piece measures 10¾" (27cm), ending with Row 2 or 4.

Knit 1 row.

Change to C and knit 1 row. Cont in double moss st, beg with Row 1, until piece measures 16" (41cm), ending with Row 2 or 4.

Change to D. Knit 2 rows. Bind off.

Turn panel sideways. With RS facing, using B, pick up and knit 68 sts across top of the 3 panels.

Knit 1 row.

Change to D. Knit 2 rows.

Cont in the foll patt until piece measures 16¼" (41cm), ending with Row 2 or 4:

ROW 1: K2, * k2, p2; rep from * to last 2 sts, k2.

ROW 2: K2, * k2, p2; rep from * to last 2 sts, k2.

ROW 3: K2, * p2, k2; rep from * to last 2 sts, k2.

ROW 4: K2, * p2, k2; rep from * to last 2 sts, k2.

Place a safety pin at the beg and end of the last row to mark end of side seam.

TOP FLAP

CHANGE TO A: Knit 2 rows.

CHANGE TO D: Knit 2 rows.

Cont in the foll patt until piece measures approx 23" (58cm), ending with Row 2 or 4:

ROW 1: K2, * k2, p2; rep from * to last 2 sts, k2.

ROW 2: K2, * k2, p2; rep from * to last 2 sts, k2.

ROW 3: K2, * p2, k2; rep from * to last 2 sts, k2.

ROW 4: K2, * p2, k2; rep from * to last 2 sts, k2.

Knit 2 rows.

BUTTONHOLE ROW (RS): K4, yo, k2tog, k17, k2tog, yo, k18, yo, k2tog, k17, k2tog, yo, k4.

Knit 1 row.

CHANGE TO C: Knit 2 rows.

CHANGE TO D: Knit 2 rows.

Change to B and bind off.

FRONT

With D, cast on 68 sts.

Knit 2 rows.

Note: The patt beg on a WS row.

Change to A and work in double moss st until piece measures 5¼" (13cm), ending with Row 2 or 4.

Knit 1 row.

Change to B and knit 1 row. Cont in double moss st, beg with Row 1, until piece measures 10¾" (27cm), ending with Row 2 or 4.

Knit 1 row.

Change to C and knit 1 row. Cont in double moss st, beg with Row 1, until piece measures 16" (41cm), ending with Row 2 or 4.

Change to D. Knit 2 rows. Bind off.

FINISHING

Sew side seams. Sew on buttons to align with buttonholes.

celebration
{ TABLE RUNNER }

I don't believe in saving precious things for special occasions. I always use my good china, and at every meal I set the table with my great-great-grandmother's silverware. I love the idea of making the act of dining a celebration. It is a simple way to show gratitude for all the blessings in your life. Whether used for a special occasion or for your daily meals, this lovely hemp table runner will bring a festive spirit to your table.

CONSTRUCTION NOTES

This pattern is designed to adorn a long dining table. However, it is easy to customize the runner to fit any table. Knit until ½" (1cm) less than your desired length, knit four rows, and then bind off.

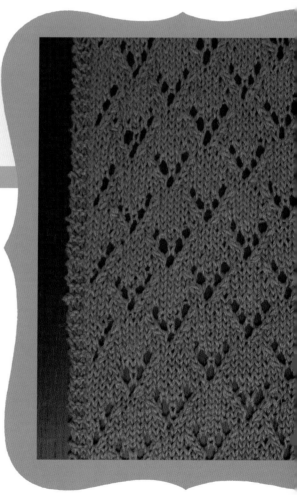

MEASUREMENTS
8½" x 63½" (22cm x 161cm)

YARN
3 skeins Lanaknits Allhemp6 (100% hemp, 165 yds [151m] per 100g)
   color Brick

Or substitute 450 yds (411m) of any dk weight hemp yarn.

NEEDLES + HOOKS
size US 5 (3.75mm) needles

If necessary, change needle size to obtain correct gauge.

size G (4mm or 4.5mm) crochet hook

GAUGE
18 sts and 32 rows = 4" (10cm) in patt on size US 5 (3.75mm) needles

TABLE RUNNER

Cast on 38 sts.

Knit 4 rows.

BEGIN PATTERN

ROW 1 (RS): K4, * yo, sl 1, k1, psso, k8; rep from * to last 4 sts, k4.

ROW 2 AND ALL WS ROWS: K3, purl to last 3 sts, k3.

ROW 3: K4, * k1, yo, sl 1, k1, psso, k5, k2tog, yo; rep from * to last 4 sts, k4.

ROW 5: K4, * k2, yo, sl 1, k1, psso, k3, k2tog, yo, k1; rep from * to last 4 sts, k4.

ROW 7: K4, * k5, yo, sl 1, k1, psso, k3; rep from * to last 4 sts, k4.

ROW 9: K4, * k3, k2tog, yo, k1, yo, sl 1, k1, psso, k2; rep from * to last 4 sts, k4.

ROW 11: K4, * k2, k2tog, yo, k3, yo, sl 1, k1, psso, k1; rep from * to last 4 sts, k4.

ROW 12: Rep Row 2.

Rep Rows 1–12 until piece measures approx 63" (160cm), ending with Row 11.

Knit 4 rows. Bind off.

FINISHING

KNOTTED FRINGE

Cut 42 19" (48cm) strands for fringe. Use 3 strands for each fringe, making 7 separate fringes for each side. Insert crochet hook through fabric, place doubled strands over hook and pull through. Draw ends through loop on hook and pull tightly. After making fringe across fabric, take one half of the strands from each fringe and knot them with half the strands from the next fringe.

Creating a sacred space for meditation provides a great support for your practice, as well as giving you a well-needed place to just relax and regroup. The area in your home where you meditate holds the energy you generate during meditation, as does the mat you sit on. As you knit this mat, repeat a favorite mantra or prayer, infusing it with the love and serenity you seek to attain from your meditative practice.

om
{ MEDITATION MAT }

CONSTRUCTION NOTES

This is a great stash-busting project! Break out your leftover skeins and bits of yarn, and design a color arrangement that speaks to you. Use this design as a template, making your own mat smaller or larger by stopping short of the number of repeats listed or by continuing on until you have reached your desired size. Use your imagination when deciding when and where to change colors around the border.

MEASUREMENTS
approx 26" x 20" (66cm x 51cm)

YARN
1 skein Lion Brand Fishermen's Wool (100% pure virgin wool, 465 yds [425m] per 226g), working with 2 strands held tog
> color #098 Natural (MC)

Or substitute 425 yds (388m) of any worsted weight wool.

approx 450 yds [411 m] of any bulky weight wool for the border
> 1 or more color(s) of your choice (CC)

Or substitute 2 strands of worsted weight wool held tog.

NEEDLES + NOTIONS
24" to 29" (61cm to 74cm) size US 10½ (6.5mm) circular needle

If necessary, change needle size to obtain correct gauge.

several stitch holders or spare circular needles

tapestry needles

GAUGE
14 sts and 22 rows = 4" (10cm) in St st with 2 strands of MC held tog

MEDITATION MAT

CENTER

Using 2 strands of MC, cast on 77 sts. Knit 2 rows.

BEGIN PATTERN

ROW 1: Knit.

ROW 2: K2, purl until last 2 sts, p2.

Rep Rows 1–2 until piece measures 16¾" (42cm), ending with Row 1.

Knit 1 row. Bind off.

BORDER

With CC and RS facing, pick up and knit 51 sts along side A. (See the Glossary for instructions on picking up sts.) Turn work and knit 1 row. Cut yarn. Put sts on stitch holders or on a spare circular needle.

Beg at end of picked up sts on side A, using CC, with RS facing pick up and knit 77 sts across side B (1 st from end of side A and 76 sts across side B.) Turn work and knit 1 row. Cut yarn. Put sts on stitch holders or on a spare circular needle.

Beg at end of picked up sts on side B, using CC, with RS facing, pick up and knit 52 sts across side C (1 st from end of side B and 51 sts across side C). Turn work and knit 1 row. Cut yarn. Put sts on stitch holders or on a spare circular needle.

Beg at end of picked up sts on side C, using CC, with RS facing, pick up and knit 78 sts across side D (1 st from end of side C, 76 across side D, 1 from side A). Turn work and knit 1 row. Cut yarn. Put sts on stitch holders or on a spare circular needle.

Cont to work the border in this fashion, picking up 1 st at beg, knitting sts from holder or spare needle, then picking up 1 st at end. Turn work, knit 1 row and then cont on to the next side.

On the 6th repetition, after the knit row, bind off.

FINISHING

Seam corners.

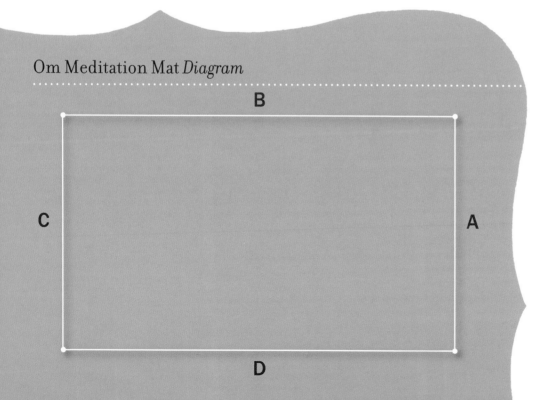

Om Meditation Mat *Diagram*

veracruz
{ KITCHEN RUG }

Brightly colored accessories always remind me of sunny, tropical locales. They lift the spirits and bring a sense of fun and playfulness to a room. While I designed this as a kitchen rug, you can use it in any room in your house that needs a jolt of color! It is sturdy enough to work in a kid's playroom or in an interior entryway.

CONSTRUCTION NOTES

Due to the weight of the fabric, the C sections are knit in two parts and then seamed together down the middle.

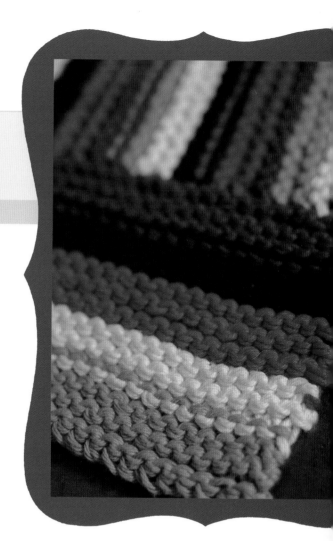

MEASUREMENTS
46" x 24" (117cm x 61cm)

YARN
2 skeins Lion Brand Lion Cotton (100% cotton, 236 yds [212m] per 113g) in each of the foll colors:

    color #157 Sunflower (A)
    color #110 Navy (B)
    color #112 Poppy Red (C)
    color #108 Morning Glory Blue (D)
    color #148 Turquoise (E)

Or substitute 472 yds (431m) of any worsted weight cotton yarn for each color.

NEEDLES + NOTIONS
32" to 40" (80cm to 100cm) size US 10½ (6.5mm) circular needle

If necessary, change needle size to obtain correct gauge.

safety pin or removable marker

tapestry needle

GAUGE
14 sts and 26 rows = 4" (10cm) in garter st wtih 2 strands held tog

KITCHEN RUG

You will be working with 2 strands of yarn held tog throughout patt.

SECTION A (CENTER RECTANGLE)

With A, cast on 89 sts. Work in garter st for 20 rows.

CHANGE TO B: Work in garter st for 9 rows.

CHANGE TO C: Work in garter st for 20 rows.

CHANGE TO D: Work in garter st for 9 rows.

CHANGE TO E: Work in garter st for 20 rows.

Bind off.

SECTION B (RECTANGLES AT NARROW ENDS OF SECTION A)

With RS facing, using C, pick up and knit 49 sts across narrow end of Section A. (See the Glossary for instructions on picking up sts.)

Knit 3 rows.

CHANGE TO D: Knit 3 rows.

CHANGE TO E: Knit 4 rows.

CHANGE TO A: Knit 3 rows.

CHANGE TO B: Knit 4 rows.

***CHANGE TO C:** Knit 3 rows.

CHANGE TO D: Knit 4 rows.

CHANGE TO E: Knit 3 rows.

CHANGE TO A: Knit 4 rows.

CHANGE TO B: Knit 3 rows.

CHANGE TO C: Knit 4 rows.

CHANGE TO D: Knit 3 rows.

CHANGE TO E: Knit 4 rows.

CHANGE TO A: Knit 3 rows.

CHANGE TO B: Knit 4 rows.

Rep from *, if necessary, until Section B measures approx 8½" (22cm).

Bind off.

Rep Section B at opposite end of Section A.

SECTION C (RECTANGLES ON LONG SIDES OF SECTIONS A/B)

Due to the weight and length of the rug, this section will be worked in 2 parts on each side and then seamed tog.

Using a marker or safety pin, mark the center of Section A. Beg at top right corner of Section B and cont across to the marker, with RS facing and using D, pick up and knit 74 sts.

Knit 5 rows. At the end of the fifth row (WS), do not turn work, but slide sts back to other end of needle. Change to B and knit 1 WS row. (You have just knit two WS rows in succession. This is the only place in the patt where this occurs. For the rest of the patt, cont working garter st in the normal fashion.)

Knit 4 more rows with B.

CHANGE TO C: Knit 6 rows.

CHANGE TO A: Knit 5 rows.

CHANGE TO E: Knit 6 rows.

Bind off.

Working from center marker to top left corner of Section B, with RS facing, pick up and knit 74 sts and rep Section C using the foll color sequence: B, D, C, E, A. Rep on the opposite side.

FINISHING

Using mattress stitch, sew center seam of Section C on each side. (See the Glossary for instructions on working mattress stitch.)

Veracruz Kitchen Rug *Diagram*

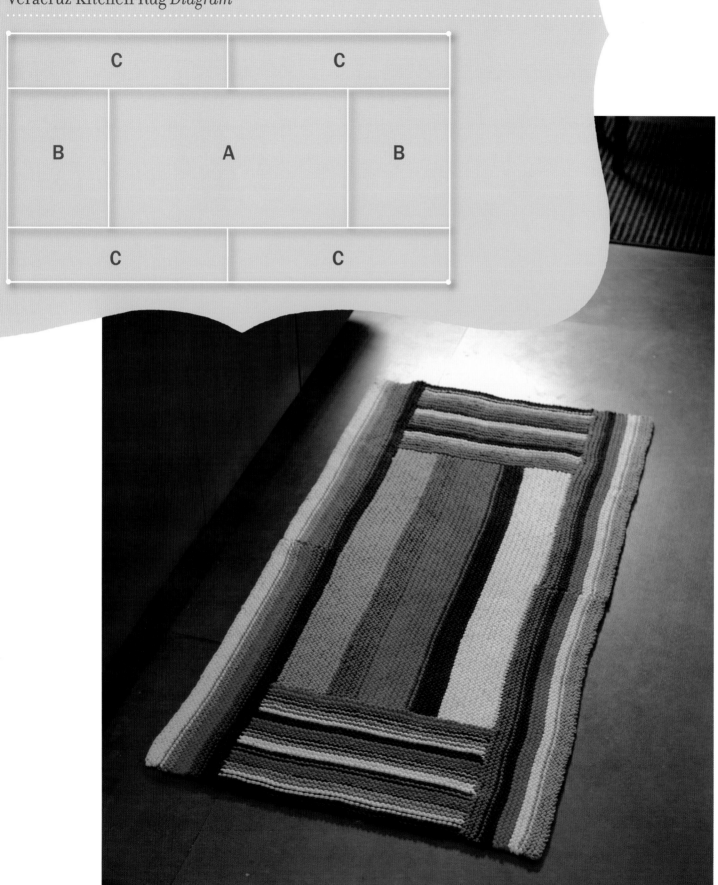

flirt
{ NAPKIN SKIRT }

To me, the mark of a great host is that he or she has *lovingly attended to even the smallest details of presentation.* It shows your guests that you find entertaining a pleasure and not a chore. Whether you are planning a backyard barbecue or a more formal affair, these lovely little napkin skirts are a delicious way to bring a bit of pizzazz to your next celebratory occasion.

CONSTRUCTION NOTES

Making a buttonhole is about as complicated as this pattern gets! You can keep your skirts sweet and simple with plain buttons or dress them up with something more ornate.

MEASUREMENTS
3½" x 3¾" (9cm x 10cm)

YARN
1 skein Lanaknits Allhemp3 (100% hemp, 165 yds [150m] per 50g)
colors Lilac and Sprout shown

Or substitute 165 yds (150m) of any fingering- or sport-weight hemp yarn.

1 skein makes enough Napkin Skirts for an intimate dinner party (about 6).

NEEDLES + NOTIONS
size US 2 (2.75mm) needles

If necessary, change needle size to obtain correct gauge.

two ⅜" (10mm) buttons

GAUGE
26 sts and 40 rows = 4" (10cm) in St st

NAPKIN SKIRT

Cast on 50 sts.

Work in St st for 1" (3cm), ending with a purl row.

NEXT ROW: K2tog across—25 sts.

Purl 1 row.

Knit 7 rows.

NEXT ROW: K3, purl to last 3 sts, k3.

BUTTONHOLE ROW (RS): K2, k2tog, yo twice, k2tog, knit to end of row.

NEXT ROW (WS): K3, purl to last 3 sts, k3.

NEXT ROW (RS): Knit.

Rep last 2 rows until piece measures 3½" (9cm) from cast-on edge, ending with WS row.

Rep Buttonhole Row.

NEXT ROW: K3, purl to last 3 sts, k3.

Knit 6 rows. Bind off.

FINISHING
Sew on buttons. Weave in any ends.

When I was a kid, I was fascinated with optical art. I would make myself sick watching those dizzying images as they appeared to sway and pulsate. Putting two strong, contrasting colors together can create the same mesmerizing appearance of vibration and movement. This fast and fun project is a painless introduction to intarsia knitting.

op art
{ GRAPHIC COASTERS }

CONSTRUCTION NOTES

Intarsia charts are read from right to left on odd-numbered rows and from left to right on even-numbered rows. Usually all the stitches on odd-numbered rows are knit and on even-numbered rows they are purled. However, for this design you will knit the first and last stitch on every row to make a garter stitch border.

MEASUREMENTS
4½" x 4½" (11cm x 11cm)

YARN
1 skein Lion Brand Lion Cotton (100% cotton, 236 yds [216m] per 113g) in each of the foll colors:

color #112 Poppy Red (A)
color #108 Morning Glory Blue (B)

Or substitute 236 yds (216m) of any worsted weight cotton yarn for each color.

2 skeins makes enough coasters for a family reunion (around 24).

NEEDLES + HOOKS
size US 7 (4.5mm) needles

If necessary, change needle size to obtain correct gauge.

size G (4.25mm) crochet hook

GAUGE
18 sts and 28 rows =
4" (10cm) in St st on size
US 7 (4.5mm) needles

GRAPHIC COASTERS

Cast on 18 sts. Knit 3 rows (Rows 1–3 of chart).

NEXT ROW: K1, purl to last st, k1 (Row 4 of chart).

Cont knitting chart as shown, knitting 1 st at the beg and end of every row (Rows 5–24 of chart).

Knit 2 rows (Rows 25–26 of chart). Bind off.

FINISHING
Using the same color yarn as in the center of the design, work 1 rnd of single crochet around the edges. (See the Glossary for instructions on working in single crochet.)

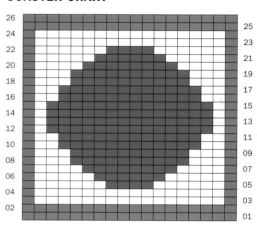

KEY

■ = CC: Knit on odd rows, purl on even rows

□ = MC: Knit on odd rows, purl on even rows

■ = MC: Knit on both odd and even rows

COASTER CHART

26 24 22 20 18 16 14 12 10 08 06 04 02

25 23 21 19 17 15 13 11 09 07 05 03 01

103

metropolis

{ STRIPED BLOCKS THROW }

As a child, I spent a lot of time sitting on my front steps and observing life around me. I can still remember the sounds, the scents and especially the colors of my childhood. Depending upon the time of day, the buildings took on various shades of pink, red and brown. For this throw, I chose colors that are reminiscent of the brownstones and brick row houses of my youth. The *Metropolis* afghan is a super-easy project with a sophisticated look.

CONSTRUCTION NOTES

This afghan is knit in five horizontal strips worked from side to side. Knit it as pictured or knit each strip with a different colored yarn from your stash, giving it a totally unique look—you might use colors that remind you of your own childhood.

MEASUREMENTS
40" x 48" (102cm x 122cm)

YARN
2 skeins of Peace Fleece Worsted (wool/mohair blend, 200 yds [183m] per 113g) in each of the foll colors:

> color Moldova Burgundy (A)
> color Buffalo Brownski (B)
> color Samantha/Katya Pink (C)
> color Ancient Fern (D)
> color Georgia Rose (E)

Or substitute 275 yds (251m) of any worsted weight wool for each color listed above.

NEEDLES + NOTIONS
size US 9 (5.5mm) needles

If necessary, change needle size to obtain correct gauge.

tapestry needle

GAUGE
15 sts and 24 rows = 4" (10cm) in St st

STRIPED BLOCKS THROW

STRIP 1

With A, cast on 38 sts.

Knit 6 rows.

BEGIN PATTERN

ROW 1 (RS): Knit.

ROW 2 (WS): K5, purl to end of row.

Rep the last 2 rows 4 times (10 rows).

Cont in est patt, knitting the first 5 sts of each WS row, as you work the foll color sequence:

CHANGE TO B: Work 16 rows.

CHANGE TO C: Work 16 rows.

CHANGE TO D: Work 16 rows.

CHANGE TO E: Work 16 rows.

CHANGE TO A: Work 16 rows.

CHANGE TO B: Work 16 rows.

CHANGE TO C: Work 16 rows.

CHANGE TO D: Work 16 rows.

CHANGE TO E: Work 16 rows.

CHANGE TO A: Work 16 rows.

CHANGE TO B: Work 16 rows.

CHANGE TO C: Work 16 rows.

CHANGE TO D: Work 16 rows.

CHANGE TO E: Work 10 rows.

Knit 6 rows. Bind off.

STRIPS 2 + 4

With C, cast on 38 sts.

Knit 7 rows. Purl 1 row (WS).

Work in St st as you work the foll color sequence:

CHANGE TO D: Work 16 rows.

CHANGE TO E: Work 16 rows.

CHANGE TO A: Work 16 rows.

CHANGE TO B: Work 16 rows.

CHANGE TO C: Work 16 rows.

CHANGE TO D: Work 16 rows.

CHANGE TO E: Work 16 rows.

CHANGE TO A: Work 16 rows.

CHANGE TO B: Work 16 rows.

CHANGE TO C: Work 16 rows.

CHANGE TO D: Work 16 rows.

CHANGE TO E: Work 16 rows.

CHANGE TO A: Work 16 rows.

CHANGE TO B: Work 16 rows.

Change to C. Knit 1 row, then purl 1 row. Knit 6 rows. Bind off.

STRIP 3

With A, cast on 38 sts.

Knit 6 rows.

Work 10 rows in St st, beg with a knit row.

Work in St st as you work the foll color sequence:

CHANGE TO B: Work 16 rows.

CHANGE TO C: Work 16 rows.

CHANGE TO D: Work 16 rows.

CHANGE TO E: Work 16 rows.

CHANGE TO A: Work 16 rows.

CHANGE TO B: Work 16 rows.

CHANGE TO C: Work 16 rows.

CHANGE TO D: Work 16 rows.

CHANGE TO E: Work 16 rows.

CHANGE TO A: Work 16 rows.

CHANGE TO B: Work 16 rows.

CHANGE TO C: Work 16 rows.

CHANGE TO D: Work 16 rows.

Change to E and cont in St st for 10 rows. Knit 6 rows. Bind off.

STRIP 5

With A, cast on 38 sts.

Knit 6 rows.

BEGIN PATTERN

ROW 1 (RS): Knit.

ROW 2 (WS): Purl to last 5 sts, k5.

Rep the last 2 rows 4 times (10 rows).

Cont in est patt, knitting the last 5 sts of each WS row, as you work the foll color sequence:

CHANGE TO B: Work 16 rows.

CHANGE TO C: Work 16 rows.

CHANGE TO D: Work 16 rows.

CHANGE TO E: Work 16 rows.

CHANGE TO A: Work 16 rows.

CHANGE TO B: Work 16 rows.

CHANGE TO C: Work 16 rows.

CHANGE TO D: Work 16 rows.

CHANGE TO E: Work 16 rows.

CHANGE TO A: Work 16 rows.

CHANGE TO B: Work 16 rows.

CHANGE TO C: Work 16 rows.

CHANGE TO D: Work 16 rows.

CHANGE TO E: Work 10 rows.

Knit 6 rows. Bind off.

FINISHING

Block strips. Sew tog using mattress stitch. (See the Glossary for instructions on how to work mattress stitch.) Weave in any ends.

One can hardly hear the word doily without the image of a fragile, yellowed piece of lace languishing on a dusty old sofa coming to mind. It is time to reclaim the doily! Bring it into the twenty-first century by refashioning it with bold, sumptuous yarn and a modern stitch pattern. You can use this darling piece of fabric to cover a nightstand or end table or to adorn a home altar.

darling

{ MODERN DOILY }

CONSTRUCTION NOTES

This simple project is knit in one piece with a single skein of yarn, which means no finishing! If you are a novice knitter this is the perfect project on which to try your hand at knitting lace.

MEASUREMENTS
18¼" x 12" (46cm x 30cm)

YARN
1 skein Lorna's Laces Lion and Lamb (silk/wool blend, 205 yds [187m] per 100g)
  color Pine

Or substitute 205 yds (187m) of any worsted weight yarn.

NEEDLES
size US 9 (5.5mm) needles

If necessary, change needle size to obtain correct gauge.

GAUGE
20 sts and 27 rows = 4" (10cm) in patt

MODERN DOILY

Cast on 57 sts.

ROW 1: K1, * p1, k1; rep from * to end of row.

Rep Row 1 thrice.

BEGIN PATTERN

ROW 1 (RS): K1, (p1, k1) twice, knit to last 4 sts, (p1, k1) twice.

ROW 2 AND ALL WS ROWS: K1, (p1, k1) twice, purl to last 5 sts, k1, (p1, k1) twice.

ROW 3: K1, (p1, k1) twice, k1, * k2tog, yo, k2; rep from * to last 7 sts, k3, (p1, k1) twice.

ROW 5: Rep Row 1.

ROW 7: K1, (p1, k1) twice, k1, * k2, SSK, yo; rep from * to last 7 sts, k3, (p1, k1) twice.

ROW 8: Rep Row 2.

Rep Rows 1–8 until piece measures approx 17¾" (45cm), ending with Row 1 or Row 5.

NEXT ROW: K1, * p1, k1; rep from * to end of row.

Rep last row 3 times. Bind off. Weave in any ends.

rustic
{ PLACEMAT }

No matter what the occasion for your meal, the placemat would do well to avoid upstaging the china and the flatware! Ideally, it acts as a backdrop for the meal that is being served, subtly complementing all the elements on the table. The *Rustic Placemat* combines two elements I love—ease and casual elegance. Even the novice knitter will feel confident taking on this effortless project.

CONSTRUCTION NOTES

This super-easy project is knit in one piece, changing colors at the middle.

MEASUREMENTS
18" x 12" (46cm x 30cm)

YARN
1 skein of Lanaknits Allhemp6 (100% hemp, 165 yds [151m] per 100g) in each of the foll colors:

> color Avocado (A)
> color Sprout (B)

Or substitute 300 yds (229m) of any worsted weight yarn.

3 skeins of each color makes a set of 4 placemats.

NEEDLES + HOOKS
size US 4 (3.5mm) needles

If necessary, change needle size to obtain correct gauge.

size E (3.5mm) crochet hook

GAUGE
18 sts and 36 rows = 4" (10cm) in garter st on size US 4 (3.5mm) needles

PLACEMAT

With A, cast on 54 sts. Work in garter st until piece measures 9" (23cm), ending with a WS row.

Change to B and cont in garter st until piece measures 18" (46cm) from cast-on edge, ending with a WS row.

Bind off.

FINISHING
Work 1 rnd of single crochet around edges, working in color A on the half worked in color B, and vice versa. (See the Glossary for instructions on working in single crochet.)

I am not easily seduced by the obviously expensive sofa or by precious objets d'art that are meant to impress. My eye is immediately drawn to the quirky and unexpected decor elements that give a room a shot of personality. I am even more thrilled when a common, everyday object is created with surprising materials or an uncommon design. With these things in mind, I designed the *Chain Maille Mohair Curtain*. This curtain is perfect for the awkward, tiny window that is difficult to dress. Or it can be cleverly displayed on a larger window between two sheer panels.

chain maille
{ MOHAIR CURTAIN }

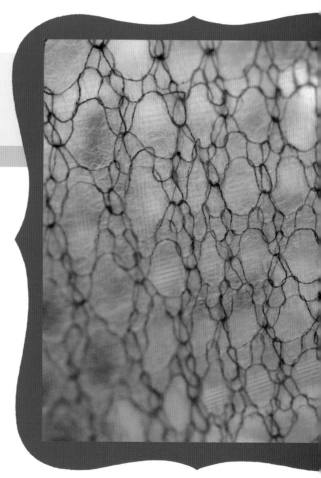

CONSTRUCTION NOTES

The curtain rod pocket is knit with smaller needles, and the body is knit with larger needles. The weight of this fabric will cause your curtain to slowly lengthen over time.

MEASUREMENTS
30" x 30" (76cm x 76cm)

YARN
2 skeins Rowan Kidsilk Night (mohair/silk blend, 227 yds [207m] per 25g)
  color #613 Oberon

Or substitute 365 yds (334m) of any lightweight yarn.

NEEDLES + NOTIONS
size US 8 (5mm) needles

size US 13 (9mm) needles

If necessary, change needle size to obtain correct gauge.

tapestry needle

GAUGE
18 sts and 24 rows = 4" (10cm) in St st on size US 8 (5mm) needles

9 sts and 16 rows = 4" (10cm) in patt on size US 13 (9mm) needles

MOHAIR CURTAIN

With size US 8 (5mm) needles, cast on 108 sts. Beg with a knit row, work in St st for 19 rows.

(WS) Knit 1 row for turning ridge.

(RS) Beg with a knit row, cont in St st for 19 rows, working the sts very loosely on the final row.

Change to size US 13 (9mm) needles.

DEC ROW: * K2, k2tog; rep from * to end of row—81 sts.

BEGIN PATTERN

ROW 1: K3, * yo, sl 1, k1, psso; rep from * to last 3 sts, k3.

ROWS 2-3: Knit.

Rep Rows 1–3 until piece measures 32" (81cm) from cast-on edge (or desired length plus 2" [5cm]), ending with Row 3.

Knit 3 rows. Bind off loosely.

FINISHING

Fold rod pocket hem to WS on turning ridge. With yarn threaded on a tapestry needle, slip st in place.

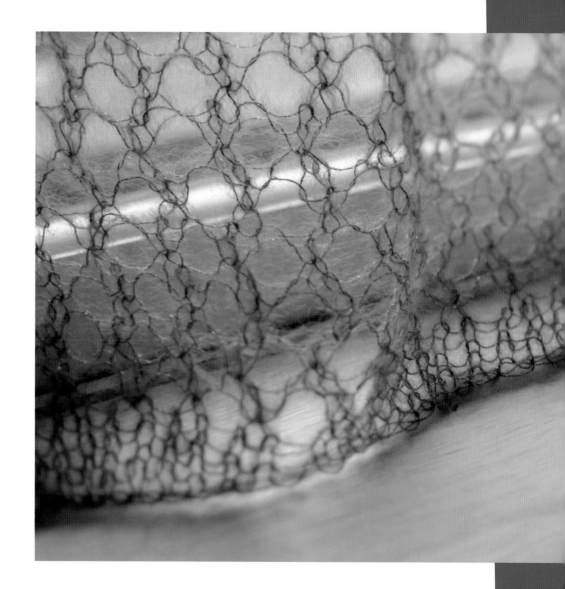

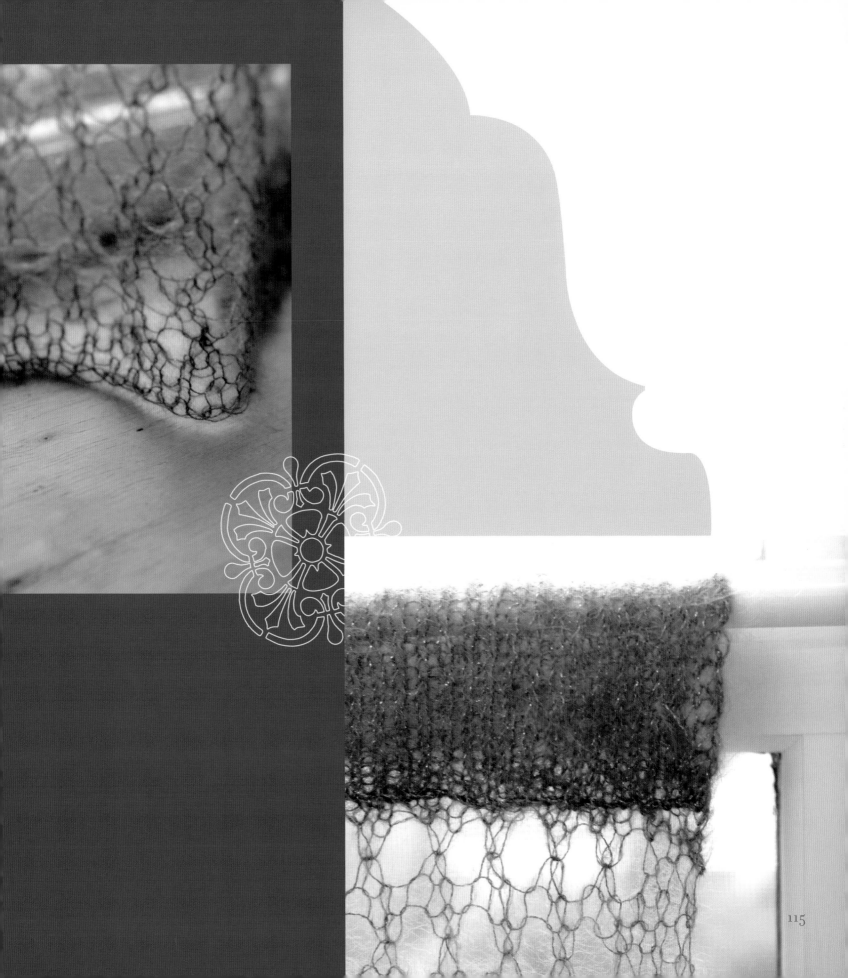

VARIOUS
+ SUNDRY

I WOULD GUESS THAT THE OVERWHELMING MAJORITY OF KNITTERS TODAY ARE NOT KNITTING BECAUSE THEY HAVE TO, BUT BECAUSE THEY WANT TO. I am sure this is even truer when it comes to creating non-wearable items. It takes a serious love for the craft of knitting to feel inspired to create something that isn't quite as necessary as a garment or an accessory. You just can't help but feel good whenever your eyes fall upon something that you have put your heart and soul into knitting just for the beauty of it. What's even better is that everyone who spends time in your space can partake in your pleasure when you play up your home décor with unique handknits.

Decoratives like table runners and afghans are great stash-busting projects. Try using the patterns in this chapter as a template for working with the yarn in your stash. Unlike garments, fit is not an issue. You can feel free to experiment with yarns that vary from the stated gauge. Fatter yarn will produce a bigger, heavier project, while finer yarns will give you something more lightweight and compact.

I love to give handcrafted gifts. Some of my favorite things to give are handknit washcloths paired with yummy soaps. It's a combination that appeals to all the senses! Like most knitters, I would never take the time to knit something like this for myself. However, I would be thrilled if a fellow knitter gifted me with a pair of these! This is definitely a present that both knitters and non-crafty people alike can enjoy. I chose hemp because it creates a sturdy fabric, and its nubby texture lends an exfoliating quality to these unique washcloths.

scrubs
{ EXFOLIATING WASHCLOTHS }

CONSTRUCTION NOTES

These washcloths are knitted in simple, textured rib patterns. Standard stitch patterns like these can be found in any basic stitch reference book. Be adventurous and try out a different stitch pattern, if you like.

SCRUB #1
MEASUREMENTS
10¼" X 10¼" (26CM X 26CM)

YARN
1 skein Hemp For Knitting
All Hemp 6
Pumpkin

NEEDLES
size US 4 (3.5mm) needles

If necessary, change needle size to obtain correct gauge.

GAUGE
24 sts and 30 rows = 4" (10cm) in pattern

SCRUB #2
MEASUREMENTS
11" X 11" (30CM X 30CM)

YARN
1 skein Hemp For Knitting
All Hemp 6
Classic Hemp

NEEDLES
size US 4 (3.5mm) needles

If necessary, change needle size to obtain correct gauge.

GAUGE
23 sts and 32 rows = 4" (10cm) in stitch pattern

SCRUB #1

With size US 4 (3.5mm) needles and Pumpkin hemp, CO 62 sts. Knit 4 rows.

BEGIN BROKEN RIB

ROWS 1–6: k3, * k2, p2; rep from * to last 3 sts, k3.

ROWS 7–12: k3, * p2, k2; rep from * to last 3 sts, k3.

Repeat Rows 1–12 until piece measures approx 10¼" (26cm), ending with Row 2.

Knit 4 rows. Bind off all sts and weave in ends.

SCRUB #2

With size US 4 (3.5mm) needles and classic hemp, CO 63 sts. Knit 4 rows.

BEGIN GARTER RIB

ROW 1: k1, * k1, p1; rep from * to last 2 sts, k2.

ROW 2: Knit.

Rep Rows 1–2 until piece measures approx 11" (30cm), ending with Row 2.

Knit 4 rows. Bind off all sts and weave in ends.

Those of us not fortunate enough to have had mothers and grandmothers engaged in needlework and other handcrafts are left with the wonderful task of making our own handmade memorables. Knitted items that get every-day use can be even more precious than heirloom quality pieces reserved for special occasions, because they serve as a constant reminder of the love and patience it took to knit them. Nothing cheers me up more than being surrounded by my handknit creations. This is the bath mat your Nana would have knit if your Nana were a knitter.

nana
{ BATH MAT }

CONSTRUCTION NOTES

At first glance, this bath mat looks like it's knit in plain old garter stitch. Look a little more closely, and you'll see that the knit-purl pattern actually creates a fabric with a corrugated look. The mat is worked with two pieces of yarn stranded together to create a thick, sturdy fabric.

MEASUREMENTS
20" X 32" (51CM X 81CM)

YARN
4 skeins Lion Brand Lion Cotton
    #144 Grape (MC)

1 skein Lion Brand Lion Cotton
    #210 Denim Swirl (CC)

NEEDLES AND HOOKS
size US 10½ (6.5mm) needles

If necessary, change needle size to obtain correct gauge.

size K crochet hook

GAUGE
Working with 2 strands held together, 14 sts and 20 rows = 4" (10cm) over stitch pattern

BATH MAT

With size US 10½ (6.5mm) needles and 2 strands of MC, CO 70 sts and knit 2 rows.

BEGIN STITCH PATTERN
ROW 1: k1, * k2, p2; rep from * to last st, k1.

ROW 2: k1, * p2, k2; rep from * to last st, k1.

Repeat Rows 1 and 2 until piece measures approximately 31½" (80cm), ending with row 2.

Knit 2 rows. Bind off all sts.

FINISHING
With 2 strands of CC and size K crochet hook, work 1 round of slip stitch around edges of bath mat, then 1 round of single crochet (see Glossary). Weave in all ends.

One of my favorite TV shows is *The Antiques Roadshow*. I was watching it one afternoon as I was finishing up Georgetown. I looked up from my knitting to glance at the screen, and I saw a woven textile that was almost identical to my project! I almost dropped my needles! The appraiser described it as "a historic Navaho blanket." This strange moment of synchronicity made me feel as though I had tapped into a collective creative consciousness where all design—past, present, and future—resides. Wouldn't it be fantastic if something you created to be used around the house survived to become a sought-after treasure 165 years from now?

georgetown
{ TABLE RUNNER }

CONSTRUCTION NOTES

Instead of knitting back and forth across the shorter width of this piece, you'll create extra-long stripes by knitting lengthwise. Switching between garter stitch and seed stitch lends texture to the table runner, and best of all, leaving long tails at each end when switching colors creates automatic fringe and keeps you from having to weave in ends.

MEASUREMENTS
64" X 8" (163CM X 20CM)

YARN
2 skeins Rowan Denim
  #225 Nashville (A)

3 skeins Rowan Denim
  #229 Memphis (B)

1 skein Rowan Denim
  #231 Tennessee (C)

2 skeins Rowan Denim
  #324 Ecru (D)

NEEDLES AND HOOKS
40" (100cm) size US 6 (4mm)
circular needle

If necessary, change needle size to obtain correct gauge.

GAUGE
20 sts and 40 rows = 4" (10cm)
in garter stitch

TABLE RUNNER

With 40" (102cm) size US 6 (4mm) circular needle and B, CO 289 sts.

note: At the end and beg of each row, leave a 6" (41cm) tail of yarn to create fringe. To secure each tail, tie it to the tail from the previous row using an overhand knot.

ROWS 1–6: Knit with B.

ROWS 7–9: Knit with A.

ROWS 10–11: Work in seed stitch with B.

ROWS 12–14: Knit with D.

ROWS 15–20: Work in seed stitch with A.

ROWS 21–25: Knit with C.

ROW 26: Knit with D.

ROWS 27–28: Knit with B.

ROWS 29–34: Knit with C.

ROWS 35–37: Knit with B.

ROWS 38–39: Work in seed stitch with A.

ROWS 40–42: Knit with B.

ROWS 43–48: Work in seed stitch with D.

ROWS 49–53: Knit with A.

ROW 54: Knit with C.

ROWS 55–56: Knit with D.

ROWS 57–62: Knit with B.

ROWS 63–65: Knit with C.

ROWS 66–67: Work in seed stitch with B.

ROWS 68–70: Knit with A.

ROWS 71–76: Work in seed stitch with B.

ROWS 77–81: Knit with D.

ROW 82: Knit with A.

ROWS 83–84: Knit with C.

ROWS 85–90: Knit with D.

Bind off all sts. There are no ends to weave in! All tails are now fringe.

TIP

The darker blue denim yarns are meant to fade like a well-worn pair of blue jeans. With use and washing, the darker blue shades might bleed onto lighter surrounding yarns. Try drycleaning if you want to keep your Georgetown looking crisp and new.

TIP

Make Georgetown wider by repeating the pattern or narrower by stopping short and casting off at your desired width.

The first things I notice when I enter a room are the artwork and handcrafted objects. They tell me about the personality of the space and the people who live there. A rigid matchy-matchy decor with no room for mischief or surprise leaves me cold, while a playful mix of styles and eras can be immensely cheerful. One or two pieces like this hand-knit cushion add warmth to a room, transforming a space from rigid and unimaginative to unique and cozy.

havana
{ CUSHION COVER }

CONSTRUCTION NOTES

Each side of this pillow cover is a two-color square. The bottom of each square is a narrow strip turned on its side, and the remainder of the square is knitted from picked-up stitches along one edge of the narrow strip. One of the squares has a triangular flap made with simple decreases. The squares are seamed together and the top is left open for the flap to cover, secured by a simple button-and-loop closure.

MEASUREMENTS
16" X 16" (41CM X 41CM)

YARN
5 skeins Araucania Nature Cotton
  #8 light pink (MC)

2 skeins Araucania Nature Cotton
  #11 dark pink (CC)

NEEDLES
size US 13 (9mm) needles

If necessary, change needle size to obtain correct gauge.

NOTIONS
1 large rounded button or button with shank

GAUGE
Working with 2 strands held together, 10 sts and 20 rows = 4" (10cm) in garter stitch

SIDE A

With size US 13 (9mm) needles and MC, CO 14 sts. Work in garter stitch until piece measures approx 16" (41cm) from cast-on edge. Bind off all sts.

Turn so that garter ridges are vertical. With CC, pick up and knit 40 sts across top edge. Work in garter stitch until entire piece measures 16" (41cm). Bind off all sts.

SIDE B

Work Side B as for Side A until piece measures 16" (41cm).

NEXT ROW: k2tog, knit to last 2 sts, SSK.

ROW 2: Knit.

Rep Rows 1–2 until 2 sts rem. Bind off and make a small loop (for buttonhole) at the point of the fabric.

FINISHING
Sew side seams. Sew on button.

mod *on* mod
{ AFGHAN }

This blanket incorporates a lot of my favorite elements and ideas. I love repetitive patterns, especially when they are knit in different colors and sizes. The range of design possibilities is endless! Everyone expects an afghan to be knit with wool. But who says you can't choose a different fiber? Knitting this afghan with a textured cotton gives it a feel reminiscent of a vintage chenille bedspread. Mod On Mod works equally well adorning a sofa or spread across a bed.

CONSTRUCTION NOTES

This blanket is made up of 20 separate knitted squares seamed together into a large afghan. Four different intarsia motifs in complementary colors create an interesting effect.

MEASUREMENTS
42" X 65" (107CM X 165CM)

YARN
4 skeins Patagonia Nature Cotton
  #203 *variegated light pink (A)*

4 skeins Patagonia Nautre Cotton
  #209 *variegated tomato (B)*

4 skeins Araucania Nature Cotton
  #4 *tangerine (C)*

3 skeins Araucania Nature Cotton
  #16 *light pink (D)*

4 skeins Araucania Nature Cotton
  #11 *fuchsia (E)*

NEEDLES
size US 9 (5.5mm) needles

If necessary, change needle size to obtain correct gauge.

GAUGE
15 sts and 22 rows = 4" (10cm) in stockinette stitch

AFGHAN

THERE ARE 4 SQUARE PATTERNS. THE BORDER COLOR IS THE MAIN COLOR (MC) AND THE CONTRASTING COLOR (CC) IS USED FOR THE SMALLER SQUARE. EACH SQUARE MEASURES 10½" X 13" (27CM X 33CM).

SQUARE 1 (MAKE 5)

With size US 9 (5.5mm) needles and MC, CO 39 sts.

ROWS 1–2: Knit with MC.

ROW 3 AND ALL ODD ROWS THROUGH 15: Knit.

ROW 4 AND ALL EVEN ROWS THROUGH 16: k2, p35, k2.

ROW 17 AND ALL ODD ROWS THROUGH 57: k7 with MC, knit 25 with CC, k7 with MC.

ROW 18 AND ALL EVEN ROWS THROUGH 58: k2 with MC, p5 with MC, p25 with CC, p5 with MC, k2 with MC.

ROW 59 AND ALL ODD ROWS THROUGH 71: Knit with MC.

ROW 60 AND ALL EVEN ROWS THROUGH 72: k2, p35, k2 with MC.

ROWS 73–74: Knit with MC.

Bind off all sts.

SQUARE 2 (MAKE 5)

With US 9 (5.5mm) needles and MC, CO 39 sts.

ROWS 1–2: Knit.

ROW 3 AND ALL ODD ROWS THROUGH 25: Knit.

ROW 4 AND ALL EVEN ROWS THROUGH 26: k2, p35, k2.

ROW 27 AND ALL ODD ROWS THROUGH 47: k13 with MC, k13 with CC, k13 with MC.

ROW 28 AND ALL EVEN ROWS THROUGH 48: k2 with MC, p11 with MC, p13 with CC, p11 with MC, k2 with MC.

ROW 49 AND ALL ODD ROWS THROUGH 71: Knit with MC.

ROW 50 AND ALL EVEN ROWS THROUGH 72: k2, p35, k2 with MC.

ROWS 73–74: Knit with MC.

Bind off all sts.

SQUARE 3 (MAKE 5)

With US 9 (5.5mm) needle and MC, CO 39 sts.

ROWS 1–2: Knit.

ROW 3 AND ALL ODD ROWS THROUGH 31: Knit.

ROW 4 AND ALL EVEN ROWS THROUGH 32: k2, p35, k2.

ROW 33 AND ALL ODD ROWS THROUGH 41: k16 with MC, k7 with CC, k16 with MC.

ROW 34 AND ALL EVEN ROWS THROUGH 42: k2 with MC, p14 with MC, p7 with CC, p14 with MC, k2 with MC.

ROW 43 AND ALL ODD ROWS THROUGH 71: Knit with MC.

ROW 44 AND ALL EVEN ROWS THROUGH 72: k2, p35, k2 with MC.

ROWS 73–74: Knit with MC.

Bind off all sts.

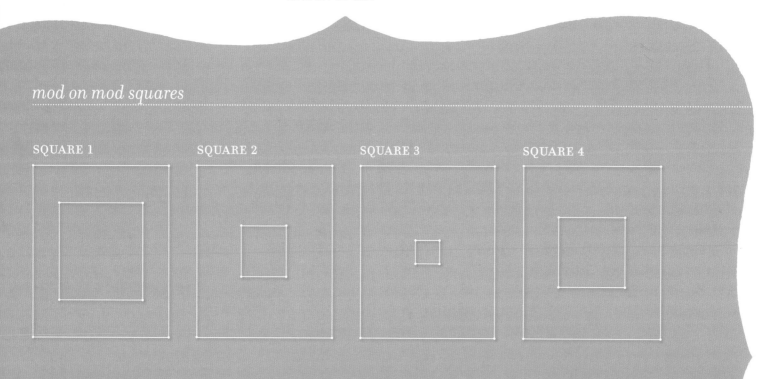

mod on mod squares

SQUARE 1   SQUARE 2   SQUARE 3   SQUARE 4

SQUARE 4 (MAKE 5)

With US 9 (5.5mm) needle and MC, CO 39 sts.

ROWS 1-2: Knit.

ROW 3 AND ALL ODD ROWS THROUGH 21: Knit.

ROW 4 AND ALL EVEN ROWS THROUGH 24: k2, p35, k2.

ROW 23 AND ALL ODD ROWS THROUGH 51: k10 with MC, k19 with CC, k10 with MC.

ROW 24 AND ALL EVEN ROWS THROUGH 52: k2 with MC, p8 with MC, p19 with CC, p8 with MC, k2 with MC.

ROW 53 AND ALL ODD ROWS THROUGH 71: Knit with MC.

ROW 54 AND ALL EVEN ROWS THROUGH 72: k2, p35, k2 with MC.

ROWS 73-74: Knit with MC.

Bind off all sts.

FINISHING

Arrange all of the squares on a flat surface, according to the diagram or as it pleases you. With a yarn needle and coordinating color of yarn, stitch squares together using mattress stitch. Weave in all ends.

TIP

Feel free to use this pattern as a template for your own unique arrangement of colors and squares. Please note that the yarn requirements listed are for Mod on Mod as designed. Yarn quantities may vary with a different arrangement.

NOTES: *switching colors*

At each color change, yarns must be wrapped around each other at the back of the work to prevent holes in the fabric. You may work with separate skeins, with yarn wound on bobbins, or with very long strands of yarn. Take time to untangle your strands every few rows.

mod on mod square layout

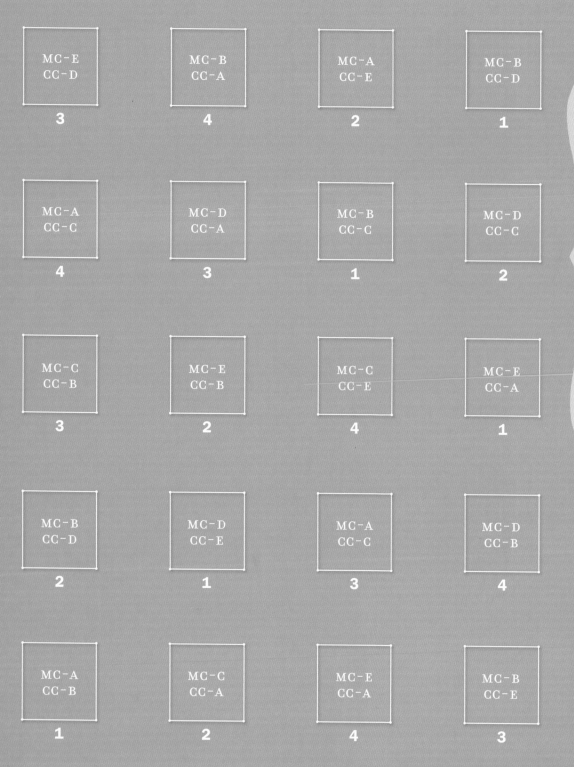

MC-E CC-D **3**	MC-B CC-A **4**	MC-A CC-E **2**	MC-B CC-D **1**
MC-A CC-C **4**	MC-D CC-A **3**	MC-B CC-C **1**	MC-D CC-C **2**
MC-C CC-B **3**	MC-E CC-B **2**	MC-C CC-E **4**	MC-E CC-A **1**
MC-B CC-D **2**	MC-D CC-E **1**	MC-A CC-C **3**	MC-D CC-B **4**
MC-A CC-B **1**	MC-C CC-A **2**	MC-E CC-A **4**	MC-B CC-E **3**

KEY

A Patagonia 203
Nature Cotton
variegated light pink

B Patagonia 209
Nature Cotton
variegated tomato

C Araucania
Nature Cotton 4
tangerine

D Araucania
Nature Cotton 16
light pink

E Araucania
Nature Cotton 11
fuchsia

MC: MAIN COLOR   CC: CONTRAST COLOR

TIP

For a different vibe, try knitting your Mod On Mod in reverse stockinette.

135

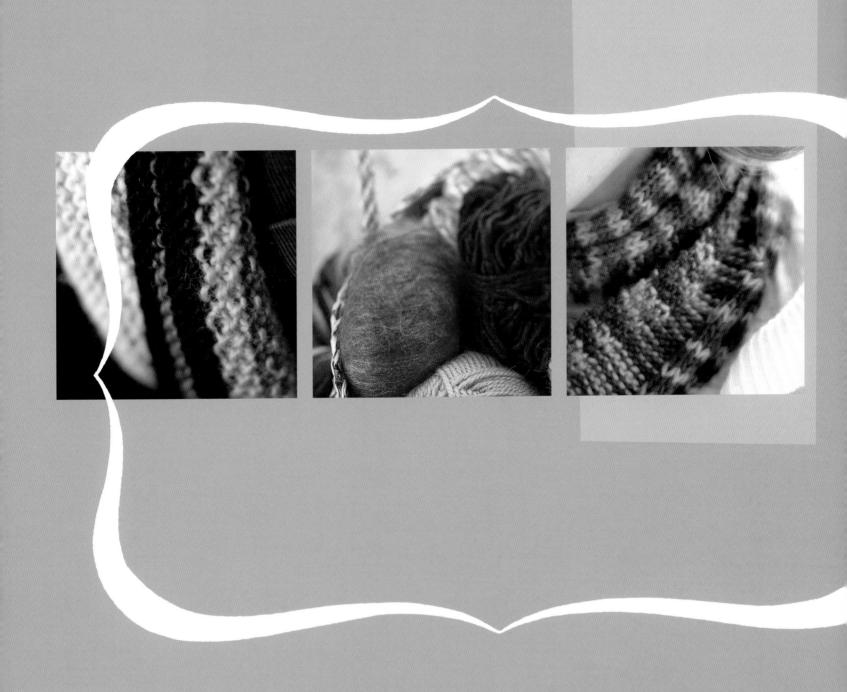

PLAYING *with* *yarn*

Wearing, gifting and decorating with my handknits is my motivation for designing. I'm always excited to wear a sweater I've made or to put a handmade cushion on display in my living space. My work is highly personal. My knitted pieces reflect who I am and grow out of my inspirations, but they are also universal because they can be worn by both young and old, the fashion savvy and the more classic dressers.

My inspiration comes from many and varied sources—everything from outsider art to fashion icons and teenagers brings me a new and fresh idea.

I particularly take inspiration from the Gee's Bend quilters and outsider artists from the American South who create amazing art from whatever materials are at hand. Like their work, mine is intuitive. For me, knitting is a meditative practice during which I allow my spirit to guide me as I choose what color comes next or how to embellish a finished piece. I just let go and release my ideas of what I think the project should look like. You will be surprised at how much fun it can be to knit intuitively. Try letting your instincts guide you by working only with the skeins in your stash to make the Everything But the Kitchen Sink striped sweater. Or you can decide where and how often to place design elements in the Lorelei tank top or the Poppy v-neck pullover .

I am also inspired by old school fashion designers like Vivienne Westwood, Yohji Yamamato, and Comme des Garcons, whose innovative use of fabric and shapes challenges and changes the very definition of fashion. Similarly, I like to turn things inside out, upside down, and on their sides to find a new way of doing things. I don't mind making mistakes because I know a mistake can be the beginning of a new design element.

I also draw inspiration from pop culture. I'm constantly exploring both new and old music, film and art, as well as the icons behind these creations. These influences saturate my consciousness and occasionally make their way into my designs (check out the asymmetrical Edie cardigan.)

Inspiration is never hard to find. When I am feeling creatively challenged I check out what my teenaged friends are wearing. They often have their finger on the pulse of what's hot on the streets. (The Austin Armwarmers are totally something my younger pals would wear!)

Of course, although creating knitted designs to fit your own personal inspirations is great, you can't put the cart before the horse. My philosophy is to first get a firm grasp on the basics of knitting. Understand that there is a "right way" and there are "other ways." Perfect the right way to do things to the best of your ability, and then loosen your hold and allow yourself to pursue "other ways." Now, by "other ways" I don't mean complex knitting acrobatics or trying to reinvent a simple stockinette. Rather, experiment with other ways of piecing together garments, where designs are placed, how a marriage of unexpected colors can create a vibrant new feeling, or how adding unexpected texture makes a design pop.

My style incorporates elements of couture and craft in a way that reflects my individuality, sense of humor, and need for comfort. I invite you to work loosely with these designs and color schemes, following your own inner wisdom to create a piece that is uniquely you!

EASY

INTERMEDIATE

ADVANCED

skill level
GUIDE

If you know the basics of knitting, you'll have no problem following any of the patterns in this book. Some of the projects are very, very simple, requiring just one stitch. Other projects require a few different stitches and techniques. Each project has an icon to let you know the required skill level.

1 STAR   All you need to know is knit and purl.

2 STARS   Up the ante a little: knitting and purling plus sewing seams together, doing a yarn over and/or working in the round. You'll also need to know techniques like simple crochet and picking up stitches.

3 STARS   Requires some fancy skills, like using a cable needle, following a chart or exercising your design skills.

HATS + SUCH

HATS AND SCARVES ARE THE BREAD AND BUTTER OF KNITTING.
EVERYBODY WANTS TO KNIT THEM, AND THERE IS NO SHORTAGE OF
birthdays, holidays and other gift-giving occasions on which they can be given to a
favorite pal or family member. They are a great portable project to toss into your bag
and knit on the bus or subway. Also, they are perfect when time or money is an issue
and you just can't commit to a bigger project like a sweater.

What I find really fantastic is that no two people wearing a hat or scarf knit from
the same pattern will wear it the same way. There are countless ways to wrap a scarf.
Similarly, some like their hats pulled down with the brim flipped back, while others
like to let them hang off the back of their heads. Everyone adds his or her own twist,
creating a completely fresh look.

When I see someone on the street wearing a handknit scarf and hat, I often wonder what the person's relationship is to the knitter. Was the hat knit by a sweetheart?
Or a beloved Grandmother? Maybe it was knit by a best friend? Regardless of who
turned out these labors of love, you can be sure that the recipient feels special every
time he or she wears them!

sidetracked
{ MEN'S SCARF + HAT }

Nothing makes a project look more impressive than incorporating different colors and patterns in an unexpected way. Your friends will think you know your way around a skein or two when they see you sporting Sidetracked! What they don't know is that you don't need a lot of knitting experience to take on this super-easy project. These earthy colors with a zing of orange are great for a man, but this can also be an opportunity to play around and choose an entirely different palette.

CONSTRUCTION NOTES

With its ribbed brim and simple decreases for crown shaping, this classic hat is the perfect introduction for knitting on circular needles. The scarf is knitted lengthwise in very long rows, alternating between garter stitch and seed stitch to create an interesting texture that complements the variegated yarn.

MEASUREMENTS

HAT TO FIT SIZES

SMALL	21" (53CM)
MEDIUM	22" (56CM)
LARGE	23" (59CM)

SCARF
6" X 56" (15CM X 142CM)

YARN
2 (2, 3) skeins Filatura di Crosa
127 Print
> #14 variegated off-white with browns (A)

1 skein Filatura di Crosa
127 Print
> #18 variegated black (B)

2 (2, 3) skeins Filatura di Crosa
127 Print
> #21 variegated tan and khaki (C)

NEEDLES
16" (40cm) size US 9 (5.5mm) circular needle

32"–40" (80cm-100cm) size US 9 (5.5mm) circular needle

size US 9 (5.5mm) dpn

If necessary, change needle size to obtain correct gauge.

GAUGE
16 sts and 26 rows = 4" (10cm) in stockinette stitch

NOTES: *seed stitch*

Seed stitch is worked by knitting all purl stitches and purling all knit stitches. Here's how it works:

FOR AN ODD NUMBER OF STITCHES

ROW 1: * k1, p1; rep from * until last st, k1.

Rep Row 1.

FOR AN EVEN NUMBER OF STITCHES

ROW 1: * k1, p1; rep from * until end of row.

ROW 2: * p1, k1; rep from * until end of row.

Rep Rows 1 and 2.

SCARF

With size US 9 (5.5mm) 32"–40" (80cm–100cm) circular needle and A, cast on 201 sts.

Work in garter stitch for 1¼" (3cm), then work in seed stitch for 1¼" (3cm). Cont to alternate between garter and seed stitch in 1¼" (3cm) increments. At the same time, when work measures 2½" (6cm) from cast-on edge, cut yarn and join in C. Work in the established pattern with C until work measures 4¾" (12cm). Cut yarn and join in B and cont in established pattern until work measures 6¼" (16cm) from cast-on edge.

Bind off all sts and weave in ends.

NOTES: *k2tog*

Knitting two stitches together as one (k2tog) is a simple way to decrease the number of stitches in a row. Simply slip your right hand needle through the first two stitches on the left hand needle from front to back, as for a regular knit stitch. Knit the two stitches as one, creating one less stitch.

HAT

With size US 9 (5.5mm) 16" (41cm) circular needle, CO 84 (88, 92) sts with B. Join sts for working in the round, taking care not to twist sts. Work in k2, p2 rib for 3 rnds.

RNDS 4–7: Cont in k2, p2 rib with C.

RNDS 8–12: Cont in k2, p2 rib with A.

RNDS 13–15: Knit with B.

RNDS 16–17: Knit with C.

Repeat Rnds 13–17 twice.

RNDS 28–29: Knit with A.

RNDS 30–31: Knit with B.

RNDS 32–34: Knit with C.

RNDS 35–36: Knit with A.

Repeat Rnds 32–36 for the remainder of the hat. Work straight until hat measures 7" (18cm) from cast-on edge.

CROWN SHAPING

RND 1:
  SMALL: Knit (84 sts).
  MEDIUM: * k20, k2tog; rep from * to end (84 sts).
  LARGE: * k9, k2tog; rep from * to last 4 sts, k4 (84 sts).

RND 2: * k10, k2tog; rep from * to end (77 sts).

RND 3: *k9, k2tog; rep from * to end (70 sts).

RND 4: * k8, k2tog; rep from * to end (63 sts).

RND 5: * k7, k2tog; rep from * to end (56 sts).

RND 6: * k6, k2tog; rep from * to end (49 sts).

RND 7: * k5, k2tog; rep from * to end (42 sts).

RND 8: * k4, k2tog; rep from * to end (35 sts).

RND 9: * k3, k2tog; rep from * to end (28 sts).

RND 10: * k2tog; rep from * to end (14 sts).

Cut yarn, leaving an 8" (20cm) tail. Thread tail through rem sts and weave in firmly on wrong side of hat. Weave in all rem tails.

NOTES: *working in the round*

If this is your first in-the-round project, you may not believe this: knitting in the round is easier than knitting on straight needles. Here's why: To produce a beautiful and quick stockinette stitch, you only have to knit. No purling! Seriously.

Before you begin, make sure that your circular needles are a bit shorter than the diameter of your project. For instance, to make the Sidetracked hat, you need needles that are 16" (40cm). Simply cast on the requisite number of stitches just as on straight needles. Hold the needle with the tail dangling from it in your left hand. Push the stitches to the end of the needle. Hold the needle with the working yarn in your right hand, pushing the first stitches to the end of that needle. Insert the tip of the right needle into the first stitch on the left needle from front to back. Wrap the working yarn around the right needle and knit your first stitch. Voilá, you're connected! Knit every round, being careful not to twist your stitches.

The illustration at right is for working in the round using double-pointed needles. You generally need to switch to dpns at the crown of a hat, when the stitches get too tight. See the Glossary, for information on casting on with dpns.

tami
{ RIBBED SCARF + HAT }

When I was a little girl, I was all about accessories.
No winter outfit was complete without a matching hat and scarf.
Now that I am a much bigger girl, I still find this essential cold
weather set really sweet! I love the sugary raspberry color, but
you can also choose a guy-friendly shade and knit it up for your
style-conscious beau! With a matching hat and scarf set, you
might just look forward to that first cold winter's day.

CONSTRUCTION NOTES

This project is an easy introduction to working with a stitch pattern and learning advanced techniques, such as picking up stitches. The scarf is knit in a simple broken rib. To make the hat, you'll first knit the brim in a long strip. Then the ends of the brim are sewn together to create a circle. The rest of the hat is knitted on circular needles by picking up stitches from the brim.

MEASUREMENTS

HAT TO FIT SIZES

SMALL	21" (53CM)
MEDIUM	22" (56CM)
LARGE	23" (58CM)

SCARF

APPROX 6½" X 72" (17CM X 183CM)

YARN

6 (6, 7) skeins Filatura di Crosa
127 Print
#37 variegated pink

NEEDLES

size US 8 (5mm) needles

16" (40cm) size US 8 (5mm) circular needle

size US 8 (5mm) dpn

If necessary, change needle size to obtain correct gauge.

GAUGE

16 sts and 26 rows = 4" (10cm) in stockinette stitch

149

SCARF

With yarn and US 8 (5mm) needles, CO 35 sts. *k2, p2; rep from * to last 3 sts, k2, p1. Repeat this row until your scarf measures 72" (183cm). Bind off all sts and weave in ends.

HAT
BRIM

With size US 8 (5mm) circular needle, CO 11 (11, 11) sts. * k2, p2; rep from * to last 3 sts, k2, p1. Rep this row until piece measures 21¼ (22¼, 23¼)" (54 [57, 59]cm). Bind off all sts. Sew up back seam.

MAIN SECTION

With size US 8 (5mm) circular needle, pick up and k84 (88, 92) sts around top of brim. Join yarn for working in the round. Purl 1 rnd. Knit next and all foll rnds. Cont straight in stockinette until hat measures 7" (18cm) from bottom edge of brim.

CROWN SHAPING

RND 1: Dec 3 (0, 2) sts evenly spaced across rnd (81 [88, 90] sts).

RND 2: * k7 (9, 8), k2tog; rep from * to end (72 [80, 81] sts).

RND 3: * k6 (8, 7), k2tog; rep from * to end (63 [72, 72] sts).

RND 4: * k5 (7, 6), k2tog; rep from * to end (54 [64, 63] sts).

RND 5: * k4 (6, 5), k2tog; rep from * to end (45 [56, 54] sts).

RND 6: * k3 (5, 4), k2tog; rep from * to end (36 [48, 45] sts).

RND 7: * k2 (4, 3), k2tog; rep from * to end (27 [40, 36] sts).

RND 8: * k1 (3, 2), k2tog; rep from * to end (18 [32, 27] sts).

RND 9:
SMALL: * k2tog; rep from * to end (9 sts).
MEDIUM: * k2, k2tog; rep from * to end (24 sts).
LARGE: * k1, k2tog; rep from * to end (18 sts)

RND 10:
MEDIUM: * k1, k2tog; rep from * to end (16 sts).
LARGE: * k2tog; rep from * to end (9 sts).

RND 11 (SIZE MED ONLY): * k2tog; rep from * to end (8 sts).

Cut yarn, leaving an 8" (20cm) tail. Use a yarn needle to pull the tail through rem sts on knitting needles. Tighten the tail to pull sts together and then weave the end in firmly on wrong side of hat. Weave in all other ends.

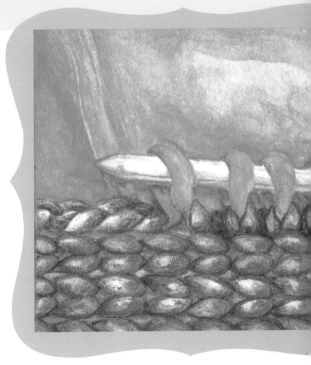

NOTES: *picking up stitches*

For the Tami Hat, you'll be picking up stitches around the top of the brim. Simply insert the tip of one needle through the edge of the fabric from front to back. Leaving about a 3"–4" (8cm–10cm) tail, wrap yarn around the needle as you would for a regular knit stitch. Bring the yarn through the stitch, creating a loop on your needle. This loop is the first picked-up stitch. Continue to pick up the number of stitches required, making sure to space them evenly.

austin
{ ARMWARMERS }

A couple of years ago I moved from the northeast to the south. The change in climate has been a huge adjustment for me. When I expect it to be cold, it's hot. When I expect it to be hot, it's even hotter. Abundant air conditioning in the summertime makes indoor temperatures just as extreme. Lightweight yarn makes these armwarmers perfect to wear with a t-shirt and a light jacket on a changeable winter day or to wear indoors at the height of air-conditioned summer. Whether you want to get warm or look cool, these armwarmers are perfect!

CONSTRUCTION NOTES

These armwarmers are really just long, skinny tubes with ribbing at either end. They are a great warm-up for knitting more complicated in-the-round projects, like socks. Knitting the first few rounds takes concentration, but after an inch or two, it's pretty effortless.

MEASUREMENTS
PATTERN AS GIVEN IS 17" (43CM) IN LENGTH, 6" (16CM) AROUND WRIST, AND 10" (25CM) AROUND UPPER ARM

YARN
1 skein Lorna's Laces Shepherd Sport
   #38 Mixed Berry (MC)

1 skein Lorna's Laces Shepherd Sport
   #45 Cranberry (CC)

NEEDLES
size US 3 (3.25mm) double-pointed needles (dpn)

size US 2 (2.75mm) dpn (optional)

If necessary, change needle size to obtain correct gauge.

GAUGE
28 sts and 36 rows = 4" (10cm) in slightly stretched k2, p2 rib on size 3 (3.25mm) needles

ARMWARMERS

WRIST CUFF

CO 44 sts with CC and size US 3 (3.25mm) dpn. Divide sts evenly over four needles and join, taking care not to twist sts. You may pm to mark beg of rnd, or use the tail from the cast on as a marker. Work in k2, p2 rib for 6" (15cm).

MIDSECTION

At beg of next rnd, switch to MC and reverse rib by working in p2, k2 rib. Work straight for 6 rnds.

BEGIN INCREASES

Inc 1 st at beg and end of next rnd and every foll seventh rnd 11 times (68 sts), working inc into pattern. At the same time, when piece measures 14" (36cm) from cast-on edge, change to CC and reverse rib by working in k2, p2 rib.

UPPER ARM CUFF

When inc are complete, cont straight until armwarmer measures 17" (43cm) from cast-on edge. Bind off all sts and weave in ends. If desired, you may work the final ½" (1cm) of the upper arm cuff with size US 2 (2.75mm) dpn to make the ribbing a little tighter.

NOTES: *personalizing your fit*

If you'd like to tailor your armwarmers to fit the exact dimensions of your arms, follow these simple calculations.

NUMBER OF STITCHES TO CAST ON FOR WRIST

Circumference around wrist bone + ½" (1cm) = A

Number of sts per inch x A = B

Round this sum up so it is divisible by 4.

B IS THE NUMBER OF STITCHES TO CAST ON.

NUMBER OF STITCHES TO ACCOMMODATE UPPER ARM

Circumference of elbow (with arm outstretched) + ½" (1cm) = C

Number of stitches per inch x C = D

Round this sum up so it is divisible by 4.

D IS THE NUMBER OF STS NEEDED TO ACCOMMODATE UPPER ARM.

NUMBER OF INCREASE ROUNDS TO BE WORKED

D – B / 2 = E

E IS THE NUMBER OF INCREASE ROUNDS TO BE WORKED.

Remember, you may need additional yarn if your armwarmers are larger than the size given in the pattern.

NOTES: *casting on with double-pointed needles*

If one of your double-pointed needles can accommodate the full number of stitches, cast all of the stitches onto one needle. If your needles are shorter, you may opt to cast all of the stitches onto one longer straight needle. Once all of the stitches have been cast on, divide them evenly between four of the dpn. To divide the stitches, hold the needle with the cast-on stitches in your left hand, as if to knit. Using a dpn, insert the tip of the needle into the first stitch as if to purl. Slip the stitch to the right-hand needle. Continue to slip stitches as if to purl until there are 11 stitches on each of four needles. The remaining dpn is for knitting. See page 147 for an illustration of connecting stitches for working in the round with double-pointed needles.

clutched
{ HANDBAG }

When I design, the project idea usually comes before the yarn selection. However, with Clutched, the yarn inspired the project. One hundred percent of the sales of Peace Fleece Worsted, in the color Baghdad Blue, is donated to Neve Shalom/Wahat al Salam, a village in Israel established jointly by Jews and Palestinian Arabs of Israeli citizenship who are engaged in educational work for peace, equality and understanding between the two peoples.

This quick project can be knit up within a couple of days, making it a great gift or the perfect way to scratch your itch for a fast knitting fix!

CONSTRUCTION NOTES

Knitted as one large rectangular piece of fabric, this purse requires only minimal assembly. Once knitted, the bottom of the rectangle is folded up and seamed to the purse opening. The remainder of the rectangle folds over the top to become a flap. Worked with two strands of yarn held together, this textured clutch is as functional as it is pretty.

MEASUREMENTS
12" (30CM) WIDE BY 6" (15CM) TALL
WITH FLAP CLOSED

YARN
2 skeins Peace Fleece Worsted
  Baghdad Blue

NEEDLES
size US 11 (8mm) needles

If necessary, change needle size to obtain correct gauge.

NOTIONS
two ¾–1" (2cm–2.5cm) buttons

GAUGE
Working with 2 strands of yarn held together, 11 sts and 20 rows = 4" (10cm) in stitch pattern

CLUTCH

With size US 11 (8mm) needles and 2 strands of yarn, CO 33 sts.

ROW 1: * k1, p1; repeat from * to last st, k1.

Repeat Row 1 until piece measures 13" (33cm), ending with a WS row.

FLAP

NEXT ROW: k1, p1, k29, p1, k1.

ROW 2: k1, p1, k1, p27, k1, p1, k1.

Repeat these 2 rows 5 more times.

BUTTONHOLE ROWS

NEXT ROW: k1, p1, k3, yo, k2tog, k19, k2tog, yo, k3, p1, k1.

ROW 2: * k1, p1; rep to last st, k1.

Repeat Row 2 five more times.

Bind off all sts in pattern.

FINISHING

Fold up bottom of bag to approx 6" (15cm). Sew side seams. Sew on buttons to align with buttonholes.

Do not block!

manta ray
{ **SHAWL** }

Whether you are cruising the flea market on a Saturday morning or meeting up with friends for a special celebration, Manta Ray is definitely the shawl to be seen in! Its dramatic look raises the bar on a casual outfit, or it can be the pièce de résistance of an elegant evening ensemble. Open stitchwork makes this versatile wrap look light and airy, but it's decptively warm. Wear it any way you like—double it up corner-to-corner, fold it in half lengthways, or just wear it unfurled.

CONSTRUCTION NOTES

This shawl is worked from corner to corner, beginning with just three stitches and increasing two stitches in the center until the full number of stitches is acheived. Continue knitting for a longer and wider shawl, or stop at your desired length if you prefer your Manta Ray short and sweet.

MEASUREMENTS
50" X 50" (127CM X 127CM)

YARN
1 skein Lorna's Laces Heaven
   #70 Vera

NEEDLES
size US 8 (5mm) circular needle,
32" (80cm) or longer

If necessary, change needle size to obtain correct gauge.

GAUGE
16 sts and 32 rows = 4" (10cm) in garter stitch

SHAWL

With size US 8 (5mm) 32" (81cm) circular needle, CO 3 sts.

ROW 1 AND ALL ODD ROWS: Knit.

ROW 2: Inc 1, k1, inc 1.

ROW 4: k2, yo, k1, yo, k2.

ROW 6: k2, yo, k3, yo, k2.

ROW 8: k3, yo, k3, yo, k3.

ROW 10: k4, yo, k3, yo, k4.

ROW 12: k3, yo, k2tog, yo, pm, k3, pm, yo, k2tog, yo, k3.

ROW 14: k3, yo, k2tog, knit to first marker, yo, slip marker, k3, slip marker, yo. Knit to last 5 sts, k2tog, yo, k3.

ROW 15: Knit.

Rep Rows 14 and 15 until length measures 50" (127cm).

Bind off all sts loosely and weave in ends.

TIP

Fold the collar back and secure the front with a brooch for a sophisticated look!

NOTES: *increases*

When you come to a yarn over in the pattern, simply wrap the working yarn around the right-hand needle and continue knitting as usual. On the following row, the wrapped yarn is treated just like a regular stitch.

There are lots of different ways to increase the number of stitches in a given row. If the pattern simply says inc 1, you choose the method of increasing that works best for you. An easy way to increase is to knit one in the front and back of a stitch (k1fb). To make this type of increase, simply insert your right hand needle into the next stitch on the left-hand needle and knit the stitch, but keep the stitch on the left-hand needle instead of sliding it off. Then bring your right-hand needle around to the back, knit into the back loop of the same stitch, and slip it off the needle. See the Glossary for more increase methods.

copperhead
{ SCARF }

I like exaggerated shapes, so when I stumbled upon this medallion cable I knew I needed to blow it up and make it even bigger! The raised cable set against a narrow background gives the appearance of a snake in motion. Hence, the name Copperhead. It can be dressed up as an elegant evening wear accessory or dressed down with corduroys and a denim jacket. Either way, it will look dangerously chic!

CONSTRUCTION NOTES

The pointed ends of this scarf are created by simple increases and decreases. At first glance, Copperhead may seem more complicated than the other scarves in this chapter. The length of the pattern may seem daunting, but if you have a row counter handy, you'll find it easy to stay on track.

MEASUREMENTS
5½" X 78" (14CM X 198CM)
AFTER BLOCKING

YARN
2 skeins Lorna's Laces Lion & Lamb
  #102 Mineshaft

NEEDLES
size US 8 (5mm) needles

If necessary, change needle size to obtain correct gauge.

two cable needles

NOTIONS
row counter

GAUGE
18 sts and 24 rows = 4" (10cm) in stockinette stitch

SCARF

With size US 8 (5mm) needles, CO 3 sts.

BEGIN INCREASES

ROW 1: k1, p1, k1.

ROW 2: p1, k1, p1.

ROW 3: Cont in seed st, inc 1 st at each end, working inc into pattern (5 sts).

ROWS 4–5: Work in seed st.

ROW 6: Cont in seed st, inc 1 st at each end, working inc into pattern (7 sts).

ROWS 7–8: Work in seed st.

ROW 9: Cont in seed st, inc 1 st at each end, working inc into pattern (9 sts).

ROWS 10–11: Work in seed st.

ROW 12: Cont in seed st, inc 1 st at each end, working inc into pattern (11 sts).

ROWS 13–14: Work in seed st.

ROW 15: Cont in seed st, inc 1 st at each end, working inc into pattern (13 sts).

ROW 16: (k1, p1) twice, k1, p3, (k1, p1) twice, k1.

ROW 17: (k1, p1) twice, k5, (p1, k1) twice.

ROW 18: (k1, p1) twice, k1, inc 1, p3, inc 1, (k1, p1) twice, k1 (15 sts).

ROW 19: (k1, p1) twice, k7, (p1, k1) twice.

ROW 20: (k1, p1) twice, k1, p5, (k1, p1) twice, k1.

ROW 21: (k1, p1) twice, k1, inc 1, k5, inc 1, (k1 p1) twice, k1 (17 sts).

ROW 22: (k1, p1) twice, k1, p7, (k1, p1) twice, k1.

ROW 23: (k1, p1) twice, k9, (p1, k1) twice.

ROW 24: (k1, p1) twice, k1, inc 1, p7, inc 1, (k1, p1) twice, k1 (19 sts).

ROW 25: (k1, p1) twice, k11, (p1, k1) twice.

ROW 26: (k1, p1) twice, k1, p9, (k1, p1) twice, k1.

ROW 27: (k1, p1) twice, k1, inc 1, k9, inc 1, (k1, p1) twice, k1 (21 sts).

ROW 28: (k1, p1) twice, k1, p11, (k1, p1) twice, k1.

ROW 29: (k1, p1) twice, k13, (p1, k1) twice.

ROW 30: (k1, p1) twice, k1, inc 1, p11, inc 1, (k1, p1) twice, k1 (23 sts).

ROW 31: (k1, p1) twice, k15, (p1, k1) twice.

ROW 32: (k1, p1) twice, k1, p13, (k1, p1) twice, k1.

ROW 33: (k1, p1) twice, k1, inc 1, k13, inc 1, (k1, p1) twice, k1 (25 sts).

ROW 34: (k1, p1) twice, k1, p15, (k1, p1) twice, k1.

ROW 35: (k1, p1) twice, k17, (p1, k1) twice.

ROW 36: (k1, p1) twice, k1, inc 1, p15, inc 1, (k1, p1) twice, k1 (27 sts).

ROW 37: (k1, p1) twice, k19, (p1, k1) twice.

ROW 38: (k1, p1) twice, k1, p17, (k1, p1) twice, k1.

ROW 39: (k1, p1) twice, k1, inc 1, k17, inc 1, (k1, p1) twice, k1 (29 sts).

ROW 40: (k1, p1) twice, k1, p19, (k1, p1) twice, k1.

ROW 41: (k1, p1) twice, k21, (p1, k1) twice.

ROW 42: (k1, p1) twice, k1, inc 1, p19, inc 1, (k1, p1) twice, k1 (31 sts).

ROW 43: (k1, p1) twice, k23, (p1, k1) twice.

BEGIN CABLE PATTERN

ROW 1: (k1, p1) twice, k1, p3, slip (sl) 5 sts to cn and hold at back of work, sl 5 sts to cn and hold at front of work, k5 from left-hand needle, k5 from left-hand needle, k5 from front cn, p3, (k1, p1) twice, k1.

ROW 2: (k1, p1) twice, k1, inc 1, k2, p17, k2, inc 1, (k1, p1) twice, k1 (33 sts).

ROW 3: (k1, p1) twice, k1, p4, k15, p4, (k1, p1) twice, k1.

ROW 4: (k1, p1) twice, k5, p15, k5, (p1, k1) twice.

ROW 5: (k1, p1) twice, k1, inc 1, p3, k17, p3, inc 1, (k1, p1) twice, k1 (35 sts).

ROW 6: (k1, p1) twice, k6, p15, k6, (p1, k1) twice.

ROW 7: (k1, p1) twice, k1, p5, k15, p5, (k1, p1) twice, k1.

ROW 8: (k1 p1) twice, k1, inc 1, k4, p17, k4, inc 1, (k1, p1) twice, k1 (37 sts).

ROW 9: (k1, p1) twice, k1, p6, k15, p6, (k1, p1) twice, k1.

ROW 10: (k1, p1) twice, k7, p15, k7, (p1, k1) twice.

ODD ROWS 11–23: Rep Row 9.

EVEN ROWS 12–24: Rep Row 10.

ROW 25: (k1, p1) twice, k1, p6, sl 5 sts to cn and hold at back of work, sl 5 sts to cn and hold at front of work, k5 from left hand needle, k5 from front cn, k5 from back cn, p6, (k1, p1) twice, k1.

EVEN ROWS 26–48: Rep Row 10.

ODD ROWS 27–47: Rep Row 9.

ROW 49: (k1, p1) twice, k1, p6, sl 5 sts to cn and hold at back of work, sl 5 sts to cn and hold at front of work, k5 from left-hand needle, k5 from front cn, k5 from back cn, p6, (k1, p1) twice, k1.

Rep Rows 26–49 13 more times.

BEGIN SCARF TIP

ODD ROWS 1–15: (k1, p1) twice, k7, p15, k7, (p1, k1) twice.

EVEN ROWS 2–16: (k1, p1) twice, k1, p6, k15, p6, (k1, p1) twice, k1.

ROW 17: (k1, p1) twice, k5, k2tog, p15, k2tog, k5, (p1, k1) twice (35 sts).

ROW 18: (k1, p1) twice, k1, p5, k15, p5, (k1, p1) twice, k1.

ROW 19: (k1, p1) twice, k6, p15, k6, (p1, k1) twice.

ROW 20: (k1, p1) twice, k1, p3, p2tog, k15, p2tog, p3, (k1, p1) twice, k1 (33 sts).

ROW 21: (k1, p1) twice, k5, p15, k5, (p1, k1) twice.

ROW 22: (k1, p1) twice, k1, p4, k15, p4, (k1, p1) twice, k1.

ROW 23: (k1, p1) twice, k3, k2tog, p15, k2tog, k3, (p1, k1) twice (31 sts).

ROW 24: (k1, p1) twice, k1, p3, sl 5 sts to cn and hold at back of work, sl 5 sts to cn and hold at front of work, k5 from left-hand needle, k5 from front cn, k5 from back cn, p3, (k1, p1) twice, k1.

DECREASE TO END SCARF
ROW 1: (k1, p1) twice, k23, (p1, k1) twice.

ROW 2: (k1, p1) twice, k1, p2tog, p17, p2tog, (k1, p1) twice, k1 (29 sts).

ROW 3: (k1, p1) twice, k21, (p1, k1) twice.

ROW 4: (k1, p1) twice, k1, p19, (k1, p1) twice, k1.

ROW 5: (k1, p1) twice, k1, k2tog, k15, k2tog, (k1, p1) twice, k1 (27 sts).

ROW 6: (k1, p1) twice, k1, p17, (k1, p1) twice, k1.

ROW 7: (k1, p1) twice, k19, (p1, k1) twice.

ROW 8: (k1, p1) twice, k1, p2tog, p13, p2tog, (k1, p1) twice, k1 (25 sts).

ROW 9: (k1, p1) twice, k17, (p1, k1) twice.

ROW 10: (k1, p1) twice, k1, p15, (k1, p1) twice, k1.

ROW 11: (k1, p1) twice, k1, k2tog, k11, k2tog, (k1, p1) twice, k1 (23 sts).

ROW 12: (k1, p1) twice, k1, p13, (k1, p1) twice, k1.

ROW 13: (k1, p1) twice, k15, (p1, k1) twice.

ROW 14: (k1, p1) twice, k1, p2tog, p9, p2tog, (k1, p1) twice, k1 (21 sts).

ROW 15: (k1, p1) twice, k13, (p1, k1) twice.

ROW 16: (k1, p1) twice, k1, p11, (k1, p1) twice, k1.

ROW 17: (k1, p1) twice, k1, k2tog, k7, k2tog, (k1, p1) twice, k1 (19 sts).

ROW 18: (k1, p1) twice, k1, p9, (k1, p1) twice, k1.

ROW 19: (k1, p1) twice, k11, (p1, k1) twice.

ROW 20: (k1, p1) twice, k1, p2tog, p5, p2tog, (k1, p1) twice, k1 (17 sts).

ROW 21: (k1, p1) twice, k9, (p1, k1) twice.

ROW 22: (k1, p1) twice, k1, p7, (k1, p1) twice, k1.

ROW 23: (k1, p1) twice, k1, k2tog, k3, k2tog, (k1, p1) twice, k1 (15 sts).

ROW 24: (k1, p1) twice, k1, p5, (k1, p1) twice, k1.

ROW 25: (k1, p1) twice, k7, (p1, k1) twice.

ROW 26: (k1, p1) twice, k1, p2tog, p1, p2tog, (k1, p1) twice, k1 (13 sts).

ROW 27: (k1, p1) twice, k5, (p1, k1) twice.

ROW 28: (k1, p1) twice, k1, p3, (k1, p1) twice, k1.

ROW 29: (k1, p1) twice, k2tog, p1, k2tog, (p1, k1) twice (11 sts).

ROWS 30–31: Work in seed st.

ROW 32: Cont in seed st, dec 1 st at each end, working dec into pattern (9 sts).

ROWS 33–34: Work in seed st.

ROW 35: Cont in seed st, dec 1 st at each end, working dec into pattern (7 sts).

ROWS 36–37: Work in seed st.

ROW 38: Cont in seed st, dec 1 st at each end, working dec into pattern (5 sts).

ROWS 39–40: Work in seed st.

ROW 41: Cont in seed st, dec 1 st at each end, working dec into pattern (3 sts).

ROWS 42–43: Work in seed st.

Bind off rem 3 sts. Weave in all ends.

TIP
Copperhead should be wet-blocked to prevent the edges from rolling.

NOTES: *cables*

Although cables may seem difficult, they're really quite simple. To create a cable, slip (sl) the number of stitches indicated in the pattern onto a cable needle (cn) and hold the cable needle at the front or back of the work, as directed. Then simply ignore the cable needle and knit the number of stitches indicated in the pattern from the left-hand needle. Rejoin the stitches on the cable needle to the main stitches by knitting them off of the cable needle. Holding the cable needle to the front or back of your work determines the way the cable will twist.

The cable in this scarf is fatter than in most other cables. The extra width of the cables is created by using two cable needles at once instead of just one.

TIP

Copperhead is shown here with the wrong side facing front. Scarves are famous for flipping from one side to the other, and Copperhead looks fabulous either way.

SWEATERS, VESTS + TANKS

I WEAR MY HANDKNIT GARMENTS LIKE SPIRITUAL ARMOR. THE COUNTLESS HOURS AND LOVING ATTENTION THAT GO INTO KNITTING A SWEATER create an energetic force field that protects me when I feel vulnerable and lifts my spirits when I feel down. Only those who have knit for themselves can understand the very special feeling you get when you wear something that has been created by your own hands.

Never underestimate the magical power of knitting! For ages men and women all over the world have been consciously knitting intentions into their creations. As you knit a child's sweater you might wish that he or she always be protected, while a lover's garment may be knit with the desire that your beloved remain faithful and true. A shawl for an elderly relative may be imbued with blessings for good health. No matter what your intention may be, the sweaters that you knit will bear the unique imprint of your energy, workmanship and love!

sloane
{ SWEATER VEST }

Sometimes you need a little knitted something to add personality to your outfit. When a scarf is not enough and a sweater is too much, a vest is perfect! Wear it with a button-down shirt and your favorite jeans for a look that is both cool and classic. Or, if you are feeling feisty, pair it with wool shorts and boots for a bolder look. Not only is Sloane stylish, she's also quick to knit. If you are looking for a fast and easy addition to your wardrobe, this project is for you. Everybody needs a little vest!

CONSTRUCTION NOTES

The front and back of this simple vest are knit separately and then seamed together. Simple shoulder shaping and no sleeves make this a great first sweater project.

MEASUREMENTS

TO FIT BUST	
X-SMALL	32" (81CM)
SMALL	34" (86CM)
MEDIUM	36" (91CM)
LARGE	38" (97CM)
X-LARGE	40" (102CM)

YARN
4 (4, 5, 5, 6) skeins Rowan Ribbon Twist
#115, Rapid

NEEDLES
size US 17 (12mm) 29" (74cm) circular needle

If necessary, change needle size to obtain correct gauge.

GAUGE
8 sts and 10 rows = 4" (10cm) in stockinette stitch

BACK

With size US 17 (12mm) needle, CO 32 (34, 36, 38, 40) sts. Work in k1, p1 rib for 12 rows.

NEXT ROW (RS): k16 (17, 18, 19, 20), inc 1, knit to end (33 [35, 37, 39, 41] sts). Cont straight in stockinette stitch until work measures 12¾ (12¾, 13¼, 13¼, 13¾)" (32 [32, 34, 34, 35]cm) from cast-on edge.

ARMHOLE SHAPING

Bind off 2 sts at beg of next 2 rows. Dec 1 st at each end of next row and every foll row 0 (0, 1, 1, 2) times (27 [29, 29, 31, 31] sts). Cont straight in stockinette stitch until armholes measure 7 (7½, 8, 8½, 8½)" (19 [19, 20, 22, 22]cm), ending with a WS row.

SHOULDER SHAPING

Bind off 2 sts at beg of next 2 rows. Bind off 2 sts, k1, turn. Bind off rem sts. Rejoin yarn and bind off center 15 (17, 17, 19, 19) sts, knit to end.

Complete rem shoulder to match first side, reversing shaping.

FRONT

Cast on and work ribbing as for back. Cont in stockinette stitch on 32 (34, 36, 38, 40) sts until work measures 12¼ (12¼, 12¾, 12¾, 13¼)" (31 [31, 33, 33, 34]cm) from cast-on edge.

NECK AND ARMHOLE SHAPING

NEXT ROW: k16 (17, 18, 19, 20), place rem sts on holder, turn. Dec 1 st at neck edge of next and every foll third row 4 (5, 5, 4, 4) times, then every foll alt row 2 (2, 2, 4, 4) times. Cont straight, if necessary, until armhole measures 7 (7½, 8, 8½, 8½)" (19 [19, 20, 22, 22]cm).

At the same time, after first neck dec, begin armhole shaping. Bind off 2 sts at armhole edge. Dec 1 st at armhole edge of next row and every foll row 0 (0, 1, 1, 2) times.

SHOULDER SHAPING

Bind off 2 sts at armhole edge twice. Bind of rem sts.

Rejoin yarn and work second side to match, reversing shaping.

FINISHING

Seam right shoulder. Using size US 17 (12mm) circular needle, pick up and k13 (14, 14, 15, 15) sts down left front, 13 (14, 14, 15, 15) sts up right front, and 16 (18, 18, 20, 20) sts across back (42 [46, 46, 50, 50] sts). Work in k1, p1 rib for 1 row, then bind off. Join left shoulder and side seams.

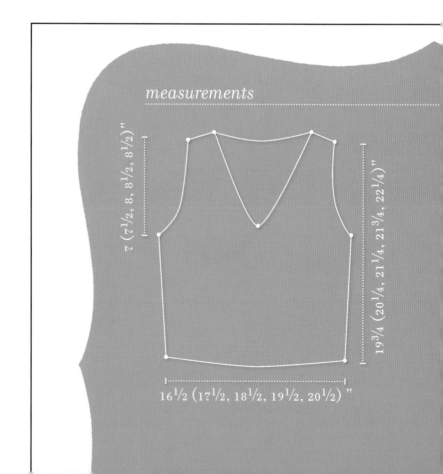

measurements

7 (7½, 8, 8½, 8½)"

19¾ (20¼, 21¼, 21¾, 22¼)"

16½ (17½, 18½, 19½, 20½)"

TIP

When working with super large needles, it can be difficult to get an accurate gauge. Consider making a smaller or larger size if you have trouble getting gauge.

When I began this sweater, I had all kinds of ideas for it. I toyed with the concept of a side-to-side construction. I thought about using several colors. On and on and on. Later, I wondered if the average guy would wear the garment I envisioned. I discussed my ideas with some men I know (and with the people who knit for them) and the general consensus was that I should keep it simple, so a man would want to wear it. Hence, the K.I.S.S. sweater was born—a simple, roll-neck pullover knit with a subtle variegated yarn.

k.i.s.s.

{ **KEEP-IT-SIMPLE-SO-YOUR-MAN-WILL-WEAR-IT SWEATER** }

CONSTRUCTION NOTES

This simple sweater is constructed in separate pieces that are sewn together at the end. Basic ribbing around the waistband and wrists as well as the natural curl of the stockinette neckline add a little subtle shaping.

MEASUREMENTS

TO FIT CHEST

SMALL	38" (97CM)
MEDIUM	40" (102CM)
LARGE	42" (107CM)
X-LARGE	44" (112CM)
XX-LARGE	46" (117CM)

YARN

11 (13, 14, 15, 17) skeins
South West Trading Company Karaoke
#284 Essence

NEEDLES

size US 7 (4.5mm) needles

size US 6 (4mm) needles

If necessary, change needle size to obtain correct gauge.

NOTIONS

stitch holders

GAUGE

18 sts and 29 rows = 4" (10cm) in stockinette stitch on size 7 (4.5mm) needles

BACK

With size US 6 (4mm) needles, CO 95 (100, 105, 110, 115) sts. Work in k2, p3 rib for 14 rows. Change to size US 7 (4.5mm) needles, and cont in stockinette until piece measures 15¼ (15½, 15½, 16, 16)" (39 [39, 39, 41, 41]cm) from cast-on edge.

ARMHOLE SHAPING

Bind off 4 sts at beg of next 2 rows (87 [92, 97, 102, 107] sts).

Working all dec as follows, k2, k2tog, knit to last 4 sts, k2tog tbl, k2, dec 1 st at each end of next and foll alt rows 3 times (79 [84, 89, 94, 99] sts). Cont straight in stockinette until armhole measures 9½ (9¾, 10, 10½, 11)" (24 [25, 26, 27, 28]cm), ending with a WS row.

SHOULDER AND NECK SHAPING

Bind off 7 (8, 8, 9, 10) sts at beg of next 2 rows.

Bind off 7 (7, 8, 9, 9) sts, and knit until there are 10 (11, 12, 12, 13) sts on right-hand needle. Turn and bind off 4 sts, purl to end of row. Bind off all rem sts. Place center 31 (32, 33, 34, 35) sts on a holder, rejoin yarn and knit to end. Work second side to match first side, reversing shaping.

FRONT

Work as for back until armhole measures 6¾ (7, 7⅓, 7¾, 8½)" (17 [18, 19, 20, 211]cm).

NECK AND SHOULDER SHAPING

Knit 26 (28, 30, 32, 34) sts and turn. Place rem sts on a holder. Dec 1 st at neck edge on next 2 rows and every foll alt row 4 times (20 [22, 24, 26, 28] sts). Work 3 rows in stockinette.

Bind off 7 (8, 8, 9, 10) sts at armhole edge once, then bind off 7 (7, 8, 9, 9) sts at armhole edge once. Work 1 row. Bind off rem sts.

With RS facing, leave center 27 (28, 29, 30, 31) sts on holder, replace rem 26 (28, 30, 32, 34) sts on needle, rejoin yarn and knit to end. Work to match first side, reversing shaping.

SLEEVES

With size US 6 (4mm) needles, CO 50 (50, 55, 55, 60) sts. Work in k2, p3 rib for 14 rows. Change to size US 7 (4.5mm) needles, and cont in stockinette, inc 1 st at each end of next row and every foll sixth row 15 (16, 15, 17, 17) times (82 [84, 87, 91, 96] sts).

Cont straight until piece mesaures 20½ (21½, 21½, 22¼, 22¼)" (52 [55, 55, 57, 57]cm) from cast-on edge.

Bind off 4 sts at beg of next 2 rows (74 [76, 79, 83, 88] sts).

Working all dec as follows, k2, k2tog, knit to last 4 sts, k2tog tbl, k2, dec 1 st at each end of next and every foll alt row 4 times (64 [66, 69, 73, 78] sts). Work 1 row. Bind off all rem sts.

FINISHING

Sew right shoulder seam

NECKBAND

With RS facing and using smaller needles, pick up and k10 sts down left front side of neck, 27 (28, 29, 30, 31) sts from front stitch holder, 10 sts up right front side of neck, 4 sts down right back side of neck, 31 (32, 33, 34, 35) sts from back stitch holder, and 4 sts up left back side of neck (86 [88, 90, 92, 94] sts).

Beg with a purl row, work in stockinette for 2" (5cm), ending with a RS row. Bind off loosely. Collar will roll outward naturally. Weave in ends.

NOTES: *placing stitches on a holder*

Most sweater patterns worked from the bottom up require that you place some of the front and back neck stitches onto a holder as you bind off the shoulder stitches. You may buy a stitch holder and slide the stitches onto it, or just use a piece of scrap yarn in a contrasting color. The stitches will be picked back up at the end to make a neckband.

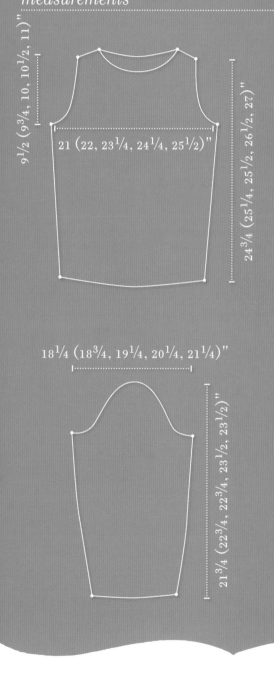

$9^{1}/_{2}$ ($9^{3}/_{4}$, 10, $10^{1}/_{2}$, 11)"

21 (22, $23^{1}/_{4}$, $24^{1}/_{4}$, $25^{1}/_{2}$)"

$24^{3}/_{4}$ ($25^{1}/_{4}$, $25^{1}/_{2}$, $26^{1}/_{2}$, 27)"

$18^{1}/_{4}$ ($18^{3}/_{4}$, $19^{1}/_{4}$, $20^{1}/_{4}$, $21^{1}/_{4}$)"

$21^{3}/_{4}$ ($22^{3}/_{4}$, $22^{3}/_{4}$, $23^{1}/_{2}$, $23^{1}/_{2}$)"

chelsea
{ DROP-SHOULDER PULLOVER }

For most of my knitting life, I didn't have much love for the drop shoulder. That is until I saw Sarah Jessica Parker wearing one in an episode of "Sex and The City" a few years ago. I couldn't believe how up-to-the-minute-hip it looked on her. Had I missed the memo? Were stylish women all over the world wearing drop-shoulder pullovers and no one bothered to let me know?

CONSTRUCTION NOTES

Since this sweater has minimal shaping, it's a perfect first sweater. And there's plenty of space over which to perfect your reverse stockinette stitch.

MEASUREMENTS

TO FIT BUST

X-SMALL	32" (81CM)
SMALL	34" (86CM)
MEDIUM	36" (91CM)
LARGE	38" (97CM)
X-LARGE	40" (102CM)

YARN

10 (10, 11, 12, 12) skeins Artyarns Supermerino
  #135 variegated orange (MC)

2 (2, 2, 3, 3) skeins Artyarns Supermerino
  #116 tangerine (CC)

NEEDLES

size US 9 (5.5mm) needles
16" (40cm) size US 9 (5.5mm) circular needle

If necessary, change needle size to obtain correct gauge.

NOTIONS

stitch holders
safety pins

GAUGE

19 sts and 29 rows = 4" (10cm) in reverse stockinette stitch

BACK

With size US 9 (5.5mm) needles and MC, CO 84 (90, 94, 99, 103) sts. Work in reverse stockinette (purl on RS, knit on WS) until piece measures 13 (14, 14, 14, 14, 14½)" (33 [36, 36, 36, 37]cm) from cast-on edge.

Place a safety pin at each edge of the knitted piece to mark the start of the armholes. Cont straight in reverse stockinette until armholes measure 8¼ (8¾, 9, 9½, 9¾)" (21 [22, 23, 24, 25]cm) from marker.

NECK SHAPING

Bind off 26 (28, 30, 31, 33) sts, place center 32 (34, 34, 37, 37) sts on holder, rejoin yarn and bind off rem 26 (28, 30, 31, 33) sts.

FRONT

Work as for back until armholes measure 5¾ (6¼, 6¾, 7¼, 7½)" (15 [16, 17, 18, 19]cm) from safety pin marker, ending with a WS row.

NECK SHAPING

NEXT ROW: Purl 34 (36, 38, 39, 41) sts, place center 16 (18, 18, 21, 21) sts on holder. Add an additional skein of yarn and work rem 34 (36, 38, 39, 41) sts.

Working each side of neck separately, dec 1 st at neck edge of next and every foll alt row 7 times (26 [28, 30, 31, 33] sts each shoulder).

Work 2 rows in reverse stockinette stitch.

Bind off all sts on both sides of neck.

SLEEVES

With size US 9 (5.5mm) needles and CC, CO 48 (48, 48, 54, 54) sts. Work in k3, p3 rib for 4½" (12cm). Change to MC and cont in reverse stockinette for an additional 4½" (12cm).

Inc 1 st at each end of next and every foll eighth row 12 (8, 4, 4, 0) times, then every seventh row 0 (6, 11, 11, 16) times (74 [78, 80, 86, 88] sts). Cont straight in reverse stockinette stitch until piece measures 25" (64cm) from cast-on edge.

Bind off all sts.

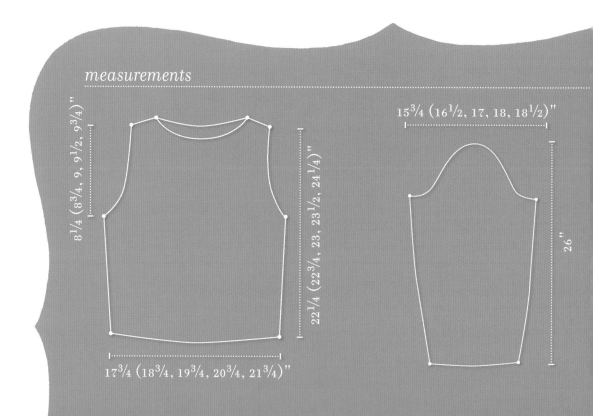

measurements

8¼ (8¾, 9, 9½, 9¾)"

22¼ (22¾, 23, 23½, 24¼)"

17¾ (18¾, 19¾, 20¾, 21¾)"

15¾ (16½, 17, 18, 18½)"

26"

FINISHING

Sew shoulder seams. Sew sleeve caps to armhole edges, matching sleeve edges to safety pin markers. Sew sleeve and side seams.

COLLAR

With 16" (40cm) size US 9 (5.5mm) circular needle and CC, pick up and knit 32 (34, 34, 37, 37) sts from back stitch holder, 16 sts down left front, 16 (18, 18, 21, 21) sts from front stitch holder and 16 sts up right front (80 [84, 84, 90, 90] sts). Join sts for working in the round.

NEXT RND: *k6, knit into front and back of next stitch; repeat from * 10 (12, 12, 12, 12) times, k to end of round (90 [96, 96, 102, 102] sts).

Work in k3, p3 rib until collar measures 8" (20cm). Bind off all sts loosely. Weave in ends.

When I designed this piece I was listening to early Bowie and The Velvet Underground. I was thinking about London's Carnaby Street in the 60s and Andy Warhol's Factory in New York City and how much the art, music and fashion of that era has influenced my taste and aesthetic. Tragic icons like Nico and Edie Sedgwick with their good-girl-gone-bad looks are permanently etched into my consciousness. This cardigan is a marriage of the sometimes severe and often playful looks the 60s underground introduced into the mainstream.

edie
{ ASYMMETRICAL CARDIGAN }

CONSTRUCTION NOTES

Knit with two complementary colors and asymmetrical shaping, Edie adds a twist to the traditional cardigan. The super-easy embroidery kicks it up a notch, giving it a fun "what's-old-is-new-again" vibe. Wear Edie with cuffed jeans and a pair of loafers for a cool, retro look!

MEASUREMENTS

TO FIT BUST	
X-SMALL	32" (81CM)
SMALL	34" (86CM)
MEDIUM	36" (91CM)
LARGE	38" (97CM)
X-LARGE	40" (102CM)

YARN

2 (2, 2, 2, 3) skeins Lorna's Laces Fisherman
#22 Turquoise (MC)

1 skein Lorna's Laces Fisherman
#6 Douglas Fir (CC)

NEEDLES

size US 8 (5mm) needles
size US 6 (4mm) needles

If necessary, change needle size to obtain correct gauge.

NOTIONS

seven ¾" (2cm) buttons

GAUGE

20 sts and 30 rows = 4" (10cm) on size 8 (5mm) needles in stockinette stitch

BACK

With size US 6 (4mm) needles and MC, CO 88 (92, 98, 102, 108) sts. Work in k1, p1 rib for 10 rows. Change to size US 8 (5mm) needles and work 4 rows in stockinette.

NEXT ROW: k2, k2tog, knit to last 4 sts, k2tog tbl, k2. Rep this row every foll sixth row 3 times (80 [84, 90, 94, 100] sts).

Work 15 rows straight in stockinette, ending with a WS row.

NEXT ROW: k2, m1, knit to last 2 sts, m1, k2. Rep this row every foll tenth row 3 times (88 [92, 98, 102, 108] sts).

Cont straight in stockinette until back measures 13 (13, 13½, 13½, 14)" (33 [33, 34, 34, 36]cm) from cast-on edge, ending with a WS row.

ARMHOLE SHAPING

Bind off 5 (5, 5, 6, 6) sts at beg of next 2 rows.

NEXT ROW: k2, k2tog, knit to last 4 sts, k2tog tbl, k2.

NEXT ROW: p2, p2tog tbl, purl to last 4 sts, p2tog tbl, p2.

Working all dec as set, dec 1 st at each end of next row, then every foll alt row 2 (3, 5, 4, 6) times (68 [70, 72, 76, 78] sts).

Cont straight in stockinette until armholes measure 7¼ (7¾, 8¼, 8½, 9)" (18½ [20, 21, 21½, 23]cm).

SHOULDER AND NECK SHAPING

Bind off 6 (6, 6, 7, 7) sts at beg of next 2 rows.

Bind off 6 (6, 6, 7, 7) sts at beg of next row, knit until there are 11 sts on right hand needle. Turn and bind off 4 sts, purl to end. Bind off rem sts.

Rejoin yarn, cast off center 22 (24, 26, 26, 28) sts, knit to end. Complete to match first side, reversing shaping.

LEFT FRONT

With size US 6 (4mm) needles and CC, CO 38 (40, 44, 46, 48) sts. Work in k1, p1 rib for 10 rows. Change to size US 8 (5mm) needles and work 4 rows in stockinette, dec 0 (0, 1, 1, 0) st on first row (38 [40, 43, 45, 48] sts).

NEXT ROW: k2, k2tog, knit to end of row. Rep this row every foll sixth row 3 times (34 [36, 39, 41, 44] sts).

Work 15 rows straight in stockinette, ending with a WS row.

NEXT ROW: K2, m1, knit to end of row. Rep this row every foll tenth row 3 times (38 [40, 43, 45, 48] sts).

Cont straight until left front measures 13 (13, 13½, 13½, 14)" (33 [33, 34, 34, 36]cm) from cast-on edge, ending with a WS row.

ARMHOLE SHAPING

Bind off 5 (5, 5, 6, 6) sts at beg of row, knit to end of row. Purl 1 row.

NEXT ROW: k2, k2tog, knit to end of row.

NEXT ROW: purl to last 4 sts, p2tog, p2.

Working all dec as set, dec 1 st at armhole edge of next row, then every alt row 2 (3, 5, 4, 6) times (28 [29, 30, 32, 33] sts).

Cont straight in stockinette until armhole measure 5½ (6, 6½, 6¾, 7¼)" (14 [15, 16, 17, 18]cm).

NECK SHAPING

Bind off 3 sts at neck edge once, then bind off 2 sts once. Dec 1 st at neck edge every alt row 3 times, then every row 1 (2, 3, 3, 4) times (19 [19, 19, 21, 21] sts).

At the same time, when armhole measures 7¼ (7¾, 8¼, 8½, 9)" (19 [21, 22, 23]cm), begin shoulder shaping.

SHOULDER SHAPING

Bind off 6 (6, 6, 7, 7) sts at armhole edge twice. Work 1 row. Bind off rem sts.

To knit two together through the back loop, insert the right needle into the back loops of the first two stitches on the left-hand needle. Wrap the yarn and knit as usual. To purl two together through the back loop, slip the right needle into the back loops of the first two stitches on the left needle from back to front. Wrap the yarn and purl as usual.

RIGHT FRONT

With size US 6 (4mm) needles and MC, CO 50 (52, 56, 58, 60) sts. Work in k1, p1 rib for 10 rows. Change to size US 8 (5mm) needles and work 4 rows in stockinette, dec 0 (0,1, 1, 0) st on first row (50 [52, 55, 57, 60] sts).

NEXT ROW: knit to last 4 sts, k2tog tbl, k2. Rep this row every foll sixth row 3 times (46 [48, 51, 53, 56] sts).

Work 15 rows straight in stockinette, ending with a WS row.

NEXT ROW: knit to last 2 sts, m1, k2. Rep this row every foll tenth row 3 times (50 [52, 55, 57, 60] sts).

Cont straight until piece measures 13 (13, 13½, 13½, 14)" (33 [33, 34, 34, 36]cm) from cast-on edge, ending with a RS row.

ARMHOLE SHAPING

Bind off 5 (5, 5, 6, 6) sts at beg of next row. Knit 1 row.

NEXT ROW: p2, p2tog tbl, purl to end of row.

NEXT ROW: knit to last 4 sts, k2tog tbl, k2.

Working all dec as set, dec 1 st at armhole edge of next row, then every alt row 2 (3, 5, 4, 6) times (40 [41, 42, 44, 45] sts).

Cont straight in stockinette until armhole measures 5½ (6, 6½, 6¾, 7¼)" (14 [15, 16, 17, 18]cm).

NECK SHAPING

Bind off 15 sts at neck edge once, then bind off 2 sts at neck edge once. Dec 1 st at neck edge every alt row 3 times, then every row 1 (2, 3, 3, 4) time(s) (19 [19, 21, 21] sts).

At the same time, when armhole measures 7¼ (7¾, 8¼, 8½, 9)" (19 [20, 21, 22, 23]cm), begin shoulder shaping.

SHOULDER SHAPING

Bind off 6 (6, 6, 7, 7) sts at armhole edge twice. Work 1 row. Bind off rem sts.

SLEEVES

With size US 6 (4mm) needles and CC, CO 38 (40, 40, 42, 44) sts. Work in k1, p1 rib for 16 rows. Switch to size US 8 (5mm) needles and MC, and work in stockinette, inc 1 st at each end of next and every foll eighth row 10 (10, 12, 13, 13) times (60 [62, 66, 70, 72] sts). Cont straight until piece measures 18 (18½, 19, 19, 19½)" (46 [47, 48, 48, 50]cm) from cast-on edge.

SHAPE SLEEVE CAPS

Bind off 5 (5, 5, 6, 6) sts at beg of next 2 rows (50 [52, 56, 58, 60] sts).

NEXT ROW: k2, k2tog, knit to last 4 sts, k2tog tbl, k2.

NEXT ROW: p2, p2tog tbl, purl to last 4 sts, p2tog, p2.

Working all dec as set, dec 1 st at each end of next and every foll alt row 14 (15, 17, 18, 19) times (16 sts). Bind off all rem sts.

measurements

13½ (14, 14½, 15, 15½)"

7¼ (7¾, 8¼, 8½, 9)"

20¼ (20¾, 21¾, 22, 23)"

10 (10½, 11, 11½, 12)"   7½ (8, 8½, 9, 9½)"

12 (12½, 13¼, 14, 14½)"

4¼ (4½, 5, 5¼, 5½)"

22¼ (23, 24, 24¼, 25)"

FINISHING

BUTTON BAND

With size US 6 (4mm) needles and CC, with RS facing, pick up and k96 (98, 102, 104, 108) sts along left front edge. Work in k1, p1 rib for 3 rows. Bind off.

BUTTONHOLE BAND

With size US 6 (4mm) needles and CC, with RS facing, pick up and k96 (98, 102, 104, 108) sts along right front edge. Work in k1, p1 rib for 3 rows.

BUTTONHOLE ROW: rib 4 (5, 4, 5, 4), yo, work 2 tog, *rib 14 (14, 15, 15, 16) sts, yo, work 2 tog; rep from * 4 times, rib to end. Work in k1, p1 rib for 3 rows. Bind off all sts.

Seam shoulders.

NECKBAND

With size US 6 (4mm) needles and CC, with RS facing, pick up and knit 5 sts across top of right front button band, 15 across right front, 15 up right front neck, 30 (32, 34, 36) across back neck, 15 down left front neck, 3 across left front, and 5 across top of left front buttonhole band (88 [90, 92, 94] sts).

Work in k1, p1 rib for 3 rows.

NEXT ROW: rib 3, yo, work 2 tog. Cont in rib until end of row.

Work 3 more rows in rib and then bind off.

FINAL PIECING

Set in sleeves. Sew side and sleeve seams. Using CC, loosely work a running stitch around edges of garment, working over two rows and under one (see Notes, this page).

NOTES: *running stitch*

Using a darning needle and CC, bring needle up from wrong side to right side of fabric. Bring yarn across a couple of stitches, working from right to left. Bring needle back through to wrong side of fabric. Skip one or two knit stitches between running stitches.

I was raised to believe that white should never be worn after Labor Day. Similarly, I am sure a few knitters may cry 'Heresy!' to find that this spring/summer-weight garment includes a little wool. This is 'The New Knitting'! Just as I learned to embrace winter whites, you, too, can expand your ideas about what to wear and when to wear it. It's important to explore our own ways to design and to knit. Blindly following patterns and knitting what everyone else is knitting has never been an option for me. If this is a knitting revolution, we should knit as we see fit!

lorelei
{ TANK TOP }

CONSTRUCTION NOTES

The bottom part of Lorelei is knit in a strip from side to side in stockinette with occasional eyelet rows and garter stitch ridges. Make this design your own by adding these variations wherever you like.

MEASUREMENTS

TO FIT BUST	
X-SMALL	32" (81CM)
SMALL	34" (86CM)
MEDIUM	36" (91CM)
LARGE	38" (97CM)
X-LARGE	40" (102CM)

YARN

5 (5, 5, 6, 6) skeins Noro Lily
   #18 muted violet

1 skein Noro Silk Garden
   #224 variegated purples and greens

NEEDLES

29" (74cm) size US 8 (5mm) circular needle

If necessary, change needle size to obtain correct gauge.

NOTIONS

stitch holders

size H (5mm) crochet hook

GAUGE

20 sts and 30 rows = 4" (10cm) in stockinette stitch with MC

BOTTOM PANEL

With MC and size US 8 (5mm) needle, cast on 56 (58, 58, 60, 60) sts. Work in stockinette stitch with occasional garter and eyelet rows until piece measures 31½ (33½, 35½, 37½, 29½)" (80 [85, 90, 96, 100]cm) from cast-on ege. Bind off all sts.

Sew cast-on edge to bind-off edge, forming a tube. Lay piece flat with seam on left side. Find halfway point (right side fold) and place marker.

TOP OF TANK

With MC and size US 8 (5mm) circular needle, beg at side seam, pick up and k156 (164, 176, 184, 196) sts around top of tube. Join yarn for working in the round.

NEXT ROUND: * p8, p2tog; rep from * 14 (15, 16, 17, 18) times. p6 (4, 6, 4, 6) (141 [148, 159, 166, 177] sts).

CHANGE TO CC and knit 1 rnd. Work in seed stitch for 5 (5, 5, 7, 7) rnds. Knit 1 rnd.

NEXT ROUND: Change to MC and *k9, m1; rep from * to 14 (15, 16, 17, 18) times, k6 (4, 6, 4, 6) (156 [164, 176, 184, 196] sts). Cont in stockinette stitch until piece measures 13½ (14, 14, 14½, 14½)" (34 [36, 36, 37, 37]cm) from lower edge.

Divide sts evenly for front and back, placing 78 (82, 88, 92, 98) sts on holder and keeping 78 (82, 88, 92, 98) sts for back on needle.

NOTES: *details*

KNITTED EFFECTS

EYELET ROW: k4, * yo, sl1, k1, psso, k2; rep from * to last 4 (6, 6, 4, 4) sts, knit to end.

GARTER RIDGE: knit 1 row on wrong side or purl 1 row on right side.

GARTER AND EYELET MOTIF

To create a garter and eyelet motif, knit the rows described above in the following sequence: garter ridge, 3 rows stockinette, eyelet row, 3 rows stockinette, garter ridge. Intersperse this motif wherever you like in your Lorelei.

SLIP STITCH CROCHET

On right side of fabric, with edge facing away from you, insert hook into top edge of stitch, wrap yarn over hook and pull through fabric. * Insert hook into next stitch, wrap yarn over hook, pull through the fabric and through the loop on hook. Rep from * to create a border as desired.

SINGLE CROCHET

On right side of fabric, with edge facing away from you, insert hook into top edge of stitch, wrap yarn over hook and pull through fabric, wrap yarn over hook and pull through loop. * Insert hook into next stitch, wrap yarn over hook and pull through both loops on hook. Rep from * as desired.

BACK

ARMHOLE SHAPING

Bind off 5 (5, 5, 6, 6) sts at beg of next 2 rows. Dec 1 st each end of next and every foll alt row 1 (2, 3, 4, 6) time(s) (64 [68, 70, 70, 72] sts). Cont straight in stockinette until armholes measure 2½ (2½, 3, 3, 3)" (6 [6, 8, 8, 8]cm).

NECK SHAPING

NEXT ROW (RS): k30 (32, 33, 33, 34), k2tog, turn, place rem 32 (34, 35, 35, 36) sts on a holder. Dec 1 st at neck edge every foll alt row 8 times, then every row 12 (14, 14, 14, 14) times (11 [11, 12, 12, 13] sts). Cont straight in stockinette until armholes measure 7 (7¼, 7½, 7¾, 8)" (18 [19, 19, 20, 21]cm).

SHOULDER SHAPING

Bind off 6 (6, 7, 7, 7) sts at armhole edge, work to end. Bind off rem sts.

Rejoin yarn and work second side to match.

FRONT

Transfer stitches from holder to needle and rejoin yarn.

ARMHOLE SHAPING

Bind off and dec as for back. Cont straight in stockinette until armholes measure 1¾ (1¾, 1¾, 2½, 2¼)" (5 [5, 5, 6, 6]cm).

NECK SHAPING

NEXT ROW (RS): k30 (32, 33, 33, 34), k2tog, turn, place rem 32 (34, 35, 35, 36) sts on a holder. Dec 1 st at neck edge every foll alt row 16 times, then ever row 4 (6, 6, 6, 6) times (11 [11, 12, 12, 13] sts). Cont straight in stockinette until armholes measure 7 (7¼, 7½, 7¾, 8)" (18 [19, 19, 20, 21]cm).

FINISHING

Sew shoulder seams.

CROCHET BORDER

With MC and size H crochet hook, work 1 row of slip stitch around neckline, then 1 row of single crochet (see Notes, page 194).

With CC and size H crochet hook, work 1 row of slip stitch around armholes, skipping every fifth stitch.

With CC and size H crochet hook, work 1 row of slip stitch around hem, skipping every fifth stitch, then work 1 row of single crochet.

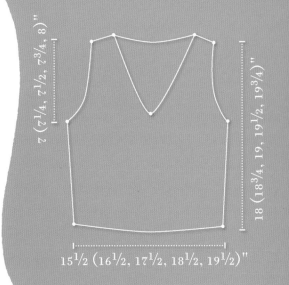

measurements

7 (7¼, 7½, 7¾, 8)"

18 (18¾, 19, 19½, 19¾)"

15½ (16½, 17½, 18½, 19½)"

Last spring I found myself staring at a beautiful pile of yarn scraps and leftover skeins that were too precious to discard, but there wasn't enough of any single one to knit an entire garment. I decided to incorporate them all into one knitted piece, using the same basic construction as for Lorelei. I chose two yarns whose palettes overlap, thus providing a vast range of interesting color combinations to choose from. As I worked on the bottom strip, I experimented with adding garter ridges and striped portions. I knit the bottom section predominantly with one yarn and the top with another.

poppy
{ V-NECK PULLOVER }

CONSTRUCTION NOTES

The bottom part of Poppy is knit in a strip from side to side. It is knit in stockinette with occasional stockinette stripes, as well as occasional rows of garter stitch. Make this design your own by using these variations wherever you like. If you decide to knit more than a quarter of this section with Silk Garden you may need to purchase additional yarn.

MEASUREMENTS

TO FIT BUST

X-SMALL	32" (81CM)
SMALL	34" (86CM)
MEDIUM	36" (91CM)
LARGE	38" (97CM)
X-LARGE	40" (102CM)

YARN

6 (6, 7, 7, 8) skeins Silk Garden,
  #84 variegated reds and browns (MC)

3 (3, 4, 4, 4) skeins Cash Iroha
  #91 red (CC)

NEEDLES

29" (74cm) size US 8 (5mm)
circular needle

size US 8 (5mm) dpn

If necessary, change needle size to obtain correct gauge.

NOTIONS

stitch holders

size H (5mm) crochet hook

removable marker or safety pin

GAUGE

18 sts and 29 rows = 4" (10cm) in
stockinette stitch with MC

18 sts and 28 rows = 4" (10cm) in
stockinette stitch with CC

BOTTOM PANEL

With 29" (74cm) US 8 (5mm) circular needle and CC, CO 56 (58, 60, 62) sts. Work in stockinette stitch, adding garter stitch ridges (as desired) and occasional stockinette stripes in MC. Cont to work straight until piece measures 33½ (35½, 37½, 39½, 41½)" (85 [90, 95, 100, 105]cm). Bind off all sts.

Sew cast-on edge to bind-off edge, forming a tube. Lay piece flat with seam at center back. Mark right side fold.

TOP OF PULLOVER

Using 29" (74cm) US size 8 (5mm) circular needle and MC, beg at right side marker, pick up and k148 (156, 168, 176, 184) sts evenly spaced around top of bottom panel. Purl 1 rnd. Knit 1 rnd.

Divide sts evenly for front and back, placing 74 (78, 84, 88, 92) sts for front on holder and leaving 74 (78, 84, 88, 92) sts for back on needle.

BACK
ARMHOLE SHAPING

Bind off 4 (4, 5, 5, 6) sts at beg of next 2 rows. Dec 1 st at armhole edge of next row, then every other row 2 (3, 4, 5, 5) times (60 [62, 64, 66, 68] sts). Cont straight in stockinette stitch until armholes measure 7¾ (8¼, 8½, 8¾, 9)" (20 [21, 22, 22, 23]cm).

SHOULDER SHAPING

Bind off 6 sts at beg of next 4 rows. Bind off 5 (6, 6, 7, 7) sts at beg of next 2 rows. Bind off rem 26 (26, 28, 28, 30) sts for back of neck.

FRONT

Transfer stitches from holder to needle and rejoin yarn.

ARMHOLE SHAPING

Bind off and decrease as for back (60 [62, 64, 66, 68] sts).

NECK SHAPING

NEXT ROW (RS): k28 (29, 30, 31, 32) sts, k2tog, turn, leaving rem sts on a holder. Dec 1 st at neck edge on next and every foll third row 11 (11, 12, 12, 12) times (17 [18, 18, 19, 19] sts). Cont straight in stockinette, if necessary, until armholes measure 7¾ (8¼, 8½, 8¾, 9)" (20 [21, 22, 22, 23]cm).

SHOULDER SHAPING

Bind off 6 sts at armhole edge twice. Work 1 row. Bind off rem 5 (6, 6, 7, 7) sts.

Rejoin yarn, k2tog, knit to end of row. Complete second side to match, reversing shaping.

SLEEVES

note: For a shorter sleeve, work 1–2 fewer rounds between increases.

With size US 8 (5mm) dpn and CC, CO 50 (52, 55, 57, 59) sts. Join yarn for working in the round, taking care not to twist sts.

RND 1: Knit.

RND 2: Purl.

RNDS 3–4: Rep Rnds 1–2.

RND 5: Knit.

Change to MC and knit 3 rows. Cont in stockinette, dec 1 st at beg and end of next and every foll eighth rnd 4 times (40 [42, 45, 47, 49] sts). Work 10 rnds straight. Inc 1 st at beg and end of next and every foll ninth rnd 7 times (56 [58, 61, 63, 65] sts). Work straight until piece measures 20 (20, 20 20½, 20½)" (51 [51, 51, 52, 52]cm) from cast-on edge.

SHAPE SLEEVE CAPS

Bind off 4 (4, 5, 5, 6) sts at beg of next 2 rows (50 [50, 55] sts). Dec 1 st at each end of next and every foll alt row 13 (13, 13, 14, 14) times, then every row 4 times (12 [14, 15, 15, 15] sts). Work 1 row even. Bind off rem sts.

FINISHING

Join shoulder seams. Set in sleeves. Sew side seams. Weave in ends.

With MC and size H crochet hook, work 1 round of single crochet around front neckline.

With MC and size H crochet hook, work 1 round of slip stitch and then 1 round of single crochet around hem (see Glossary).

measurements

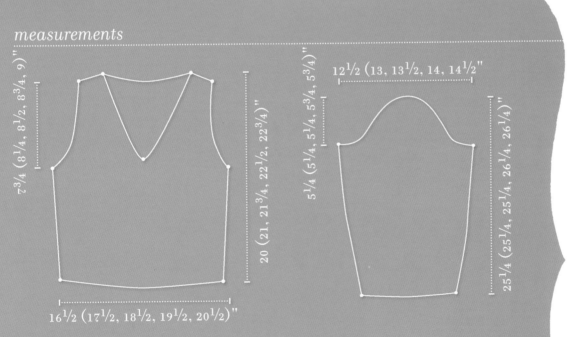

$7^3/4$ ($8^1/4$, $8^1/2$, $8^3/4$, 9)"

20 (21, $21^3/4$, $22^1/2$, $22^3/4$)"

$16^1/2$ ($17^1/2$, $18^1/2$, $19^1/2$, $20^1/2$)"

$12^1/2$ (13, $13^1/2$, 14, $14^1/2$)"

$5^1/4$ ($5^1/4$, $5^1/4$, $5^3/4$, $5^3/4$)"

$25^1/4$ ($25^1/4$, $25^1/4$, $26^1/4$, $26^1/4$)"

I am a jeans and boots kind of girl, so I expect my sweaters to make a bold statement. And nothing makes a statement like color! I knit the Everything But The Kitchen Sink pullover with about 37 different colors and textures of predominantly aran weight yarns. The more colors and textures, the better! For this design, I suggest a minimum of 18 different shades. You can stick to one color family or you can use every color that appeals to you.

everything
but the kitchen sink
{ STRIPED SWEATER }

CONSTRUCTION NOTES

The yardage of each yarn can vary from enough for one round to a full skein. In order to keep gauge, the majority of yarns should be the same weight. You can knit an occasional round with a yarn that is slightly lighter or heavier. Occasional deviation from gauge produces an interesting texture. However, you should not use these yarns for more than two rounds at a time.

MEASUREMENTS

TO FIT BUST

X-SMALL	32" (81CM)
SMALL	34" (86CM)
MEDIUM	36" (91CM)
LARGE	38" (97CM)
X-LARGE	40" (102CM)

YARN
approx 1175 (1250, 1320, 1425, 1510) yards of aran weight yarn

SOME YARNS USED IN THIS SWEATER:
South West Trading Company Karaoke
   #289 Bluezzz

Noro Kureyon
   #166 variegated blue, purple, green

Debbie Bliss Merino Aran
   #208 periwinkle
   #702 navy

Berroco Air
   #3140 variegated blues

Berroco Medley
   #8913 variegated purples

Alchemy Yarns Lone Star
   Deep Sea

NEEDLES
29" (74cm) size US 8 (5mm) circular needle

size US 8 (5mm) dpn

24" (60cm) size US 7 (4.5mm) circular needle

If necessary, change needle size to obtain correct gauge.

NOTIONS
stitch holders

GAUGE
18 sts and 28 rows = 4" (10cm) in stockinette on size US 8 (5mm) needles

note: This garment is knit in the round from the bottom up to the armholes, where the work is divided for front and back. The sleeves are knit in the round as well. Constructing a sweater in this way makes it virtually seamless—practically zero sewing things together at the end. Just a little bit of stitching under the arms, and you're done.

BODY

CO 144 (152, 160, 172, 180) sts with size US 8 (5mm) circular needle. Join sts for working in the rnd, taking care not to twist sts. Work in k2, p2 rib for 7" (18cm). Cont in stockinette until entire piece measures 12 (12½, 12½, 13, 13)" (30 [32, 32, 33, 33]cm) from cast-on edge.

SEPARATE FRONT AND BACK

Place 72 (76, 80, 86, 90) sts for front of garment on stitch holder. Leave rem 72 (76, 80, 86, 90) sts on needle.

BACK
RAGLAN SHAPING

Bind off 5 sts at beg of next 2 rows.

DECREASE AS FOLLOWS: On knit rows, k1, ssk, knit to last 3 sts, k2tog, k1. On purl rows, p1, p2tog tbl, purl to last 3 sts, p2tog, p1.

Dec 1 st at each end of every third row 3 (3, 5, 5, 5) times, then every other row 3 (15, 18, 20) times, then every alt row 14 (16, 15, 18, 20) times. Place rem 26 (26, 27, 27, 29) sts on a holder.

FRONT

Transfer sts from holder onto needle.

RAGLAN SHAPING

Bind off and decrease as for back until 40 (40, 42, 42, 44) sts rem.

NECK SHAPING

NEXT RS ROW: Work in established pattern until there are 13 (13, 14, 14, 14) sts on right-hand needle. Turn. Place rem 26 (26, 27, 27, 29) sts on holder.

Cont raglan decreases at armhole side as established. At the same time, dec 1 st at neck edge of next row, then every other row 4 (4, 5, 5, 5) times. Place rem 2 sts on holder.

Leave center 12 (12, 12, 14, 14) sts on holder and place rem 14 (14, 15, 15, 15) sts onto needle. Rejoin yarn, knit to end. Complete to match first side.

NOTES: *slip, slip, knit*

SLIP, SLIP, KNIT

To create a left-slanting decrease, slip the first stitch as if to knit, slip the second stitch as if to knit, and then bring the right needle through both stitches from front to back and knit the two stitches together.

See the Glossary to read about other ways of creating a decrease in the knitted fabric.

JOINING IN NEW YARN

When joining a new yarn, overlap it with the previous yarn and knit with both for three or four stitches. Then cut the first yarn, leaving a 2" (5cm) tail, and continue knitting with the new yarn.

measurements

$5^{1}/_{2}$ $(6, 6^{1}/_{2}, 7^{1}/_{2}, 8)$"

$17^{1}/_{2}$ $(18^{1}/_{2}, 19, 20^{1}/_{2}, 21)$"

16 $(17, 18, 19, 20)$"

11 $(12, 12^{1}/_{2}, 13, 13^{3}/_{4})$"

24 $(24^{1}/_{2}, 25^{1}/_{2}, 26^{1}/_{2}, 27^{1}/_{2})$"

203

SLEEVES

Cast on 40 (44, 44, 44, 48) sts on size US 8 (5mm) dpn. Work in k2, p2 rib for 4" (10cm). Inc 1 st at beg and end of next and every foll fourteenth rnd 4 (4, 5, 6, 6) times, working inc into pattern (50 [54, 56, 58, 62] sts). At the same time, when sleeve measures 7½" (19cm), change to stockinette stitch.

When increases are complete, work straight until sleeve measures 18½ (19, 19, 19½, 19½)" (47 [48, 48, 50, 50]cm) from cast-on edge.

RAGLAN SHAPING

Bind off 5 sts at beg of next 2 rows. Dec 1 st at each end as indicated for back every third row 3 (3, 5, 9, 9) times, then every alt row 14 (16, 15, 12, 14) times. Place rem 6 sts on holder.

FINISHING

Sew raglan seams.

COLLAR

With size US 7 (4.5mm) circular needle, k26 (26, 28, 28, 30) sts from back neck holder, knit 6 sts from left sleeve holder, knit 2 sts from front holder, pick up and k11 (11, 12, 11, 12) sts down left front of neck, k12 (12, 12, 14, 14) sts from center front holder, knit 2 sts from front holder, pick up and k11 (11, 12, 11, 12) sts up right front of neck, k2 sts from front holder, knit 6 sts from right sleeve holder (76 [76, 80, 80, 84] sts). Join for working in the round. Work in k2, p2 rib for 8 rnds. Loosely bind off all sts in pattern. Weave in ends.

As a woman whose sole experience with babies is limited to the four-legged kind, I have fairly over-the-top ideas about how little ones should be clothed. Parents are sure to provide plenty of clothing that can survive everyday wear and tear. My job is to provide a stand-out addition to their collection of bibs and onesies. I think of myself as the eccentric godmother who gifts a child with an elegant outfit destined to be a family heirloom. This special garment requires a little extra care, but isn't the baby in your life worth it?

baby a
{ BABY'S HAT + CARDIGAN }

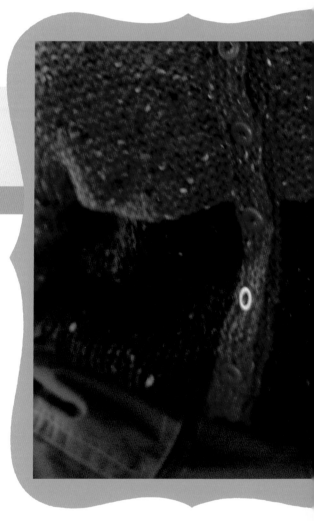

CONSTRUCTION NOTES

The beauty of garter stitch is highly underrated! This purl-free cardigan is worked in side-to-side strips, then stitches are picked up across the top edge and the garment is completed in the usual fashion.

MEASUREMENTS

SWEATER TO FIT AGE

6–9 MOS	22½" (58CM)
9–12 MOS	23½" (60CM)
12–18 MOS	24½" (62CM)

HAT TO FIT AGE

6–9 MOS	14" (36CM)
9–12 MOS	16" (41CM)
12–18 MOS	18" (46CM)

YARN

2 (3, 3) skeins Rowan Felted Tweed
　　#154 Ginger (MC)

1 skein Rowan Felted Tweed
　　#133 Midnight (MC)

NEEDLES

size US 6 (4mm) needles

size US 4 (3.5mm) needles

size US 5 (3.75mm) dpn

size US 6 (4mm) dpn

If necessary, change needle size to obtain correct gauge.

NOTIONS

six ½" (1cm) buttons

size F (4mm) crochet hook

GAUGE

22 sts and 44 rows = 4" (10cm) on size 6 (4mm) needles in garter stitch

HAT

With CC and size US 5 (3.75mm) dpn, cast on 78 (88, 100) sts. Divide sts evenly over 4 needles and join, taking care not to twist sts. Pm to mark beg of rnd, or use the cast-on tail as marker. Work in k1, p1 rib for 5 rounds.

Switch to MC and size US 6 (4mm) dpn and knit 1 rnd, purl 1 rnd. Cont in garter stitch as established (alternating between knit 1 rnd and purl 1 rnd) until hat measures 4 (5, 6)" (10 [13, 15]cm), ending with a knit row.

NOTES: *placing a marker*

Sometimes a pattern calls for you to place a marker (pm). Markers are generally small plastic rings that slide onto a needle and rest in between stitches, marking a certain spot. When working in the round, you can use a marker to indicate the beginning of each round. If you don't have markers on hand, cut small pieces of scrap yarn in a contrasting color. Tie the scrap yarn in the indicated spot in a loose knot.

See the Glossary to read about other ways that stitch markers are used.

CROWN SHAPING

RND 1: * k9, k2 tog; rep from * to end of rnd (70 [80, 90] sts).

RND 2: Purl.

RND 3: * k8, k2 tog; rep from * to end of rnd (63 [72, 81] sts).

RND 4: Purl.

RND 5: * k7, k2 tog; rep from * to end of rnd (56 [64, 72] sts).

RND 6: Purl.

RND 7: * k6, k2 tog; rep from * to end of rnd (49 [56, 63] sts).

RND 8: Purl.

RND 9: * k5, k2 tog; rep from * to end of rnd (42 [48, 54] sts).

RND 10: Purl.

RND 11: * k4, k2 tog; rep from * to end of rnd (35 [40, 45] sts).

RND 12: Purl.

RND 13: * k3, k2 tog; rep from * to end of rnd (28 [32, 36] sts).

RND 14: Purl.

RND 15: * k2, k2 tog; rep from * to end of rnd (21 [24, 27] sts).

RND 16: Purl.

RND 17: * k1, k2 tog (14[16, 18] sts).

RND 18: * p2tog; rep from * to end of rnd (7 [8,9] sts).

Switch to CC, and work 6 (8, 10) rows in garter stitch.

Cut yarn, pull through rem sts, then through top of hat and secure.

CARDIGAN BACK

With CC and size US 6 (4mm) needles, CO 34 (36, 38) sts. Work in garter stitch for 11 (11½, 12)" (28 [29, 31]cm). Bind off all sts.

Turn fabric so the garter ridges are vertical. With MC and size US 6 (4mm) needles, pick up and k60 (64, 68) sts across top of fabric. Work in garter stitch until piece measures 10¼ (11, 12)" (26 [28, 31]cm) from bottom edge.

Bind off 15 (17, 19) sts at beg of next 2 rows. Bind off rem sts.

LEFT FRONT

With CC and size 6 needles, CO 34 (36, 38) sts. Work in garter stitch for 5½ (5¾, 6)" (14 [15, 16]cm). Bind off all sts.

Turn fabric so the garter ridges are vertical. With MC and size 6 needles, pick up and knit 30 (32, 34) sts across top of fabric. Work in garter stitch until piece measures 9½ (10¼, 11¼)" (24 [26, 29]cm) from bottom edge, ending with a right side row.

NECK SHAPING

At beg of next row, bind off 7 sts. Dec 1 st at neck edge every row 8 times. Bind off rem sts.

RIGHT FRONT

Work as for left front, reversing neck shaping.

SLEEVES

With MC and size US 6 (4mm) needles, CO 35 (38, 42) sts. Work in garter stitch for 1¼" (3cm). Inc 1 st at each end of next and every foll seventh row 7 times (51 [54, 58] sts). Work straight until sleeve measures 6½ (7, 7½)" (17 [18, 19]cm). Bind off all sts.

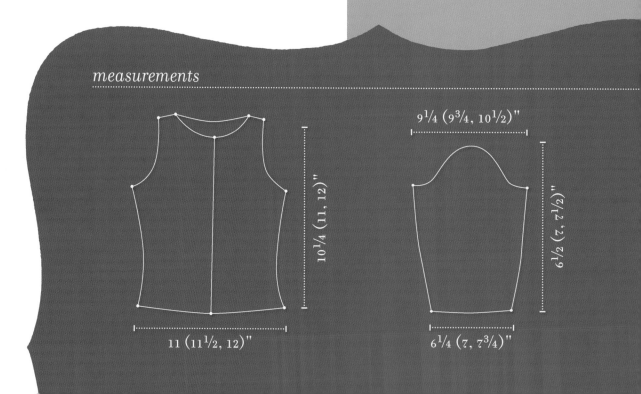

measurements

9¼ (9¾, 10½)"

10¼ (11, 12)"

11 (11½, 12)"

6½ (7, 7½)"

6¼ (7, 7¾)"

FINISHING

BUTTON BAND

With size US 4 (3.5mm) needle and MC, with RS facing, pick up and k54 (59, 64) sts along left front edge.

Work in garter stitch for 6 rows. Bind off all sts.

BUTTONHOLE BAND

With size US 4 (3.5mm) needle and MC, with RS facing, pick up and k54 (59, 64) sts along right front edge. Work in garter stitch for 2 rows.

BUTTONHOLE ROW: k3, * yo, k2tog, k7 (8, 9); rep from * 5 times. yo, k2tog, k4.

Work 3 rows in garter stitch. Bind off all sts.

PIECE TOGETHER

Sew sleeves to armhole edges. Sew sleeve and side seams, placing "armpit" at start of MC in body piece. Sew on buttons opposite buttonholes. Weave in ends.

With size F crochet hook and MC, work 1 row of single crochet around neck edge and sleeve cuffs (see Glossary for specific instructions on single crochet).

When a student of mine was asked why she didn't knit a sweater her granddaughter could grow into, she replied, "I don't want it to look terrible by the time it actually fits her." This struck me as the smartest thing I'd heard about knitting for kids. The general consensus among knitters is that kids should get as much wear as possible out of a garment. However, they don't seem to consider that it could be outworn by the time it fits. Or that it may look like a paper sack. Fitting in is hard enough for kids, don't make them suffer by forcing them to wear bad knitting!

stripey
{ KID'S SWEATER + HAT }

CONSTRUCTION NOTES

This sweater is made in separate pieces that are sewn together into a sweater. Like Lorelei and Poppy (pages 192 and 196), this sweater begins with a bottom panel from which stitches are picked up. However, instead of working in the round, you'll knit two separate panels and pick up stitches to work each piece flat.

MEASUREMENTS

SWEATER TO FIT AGE

2–3 YRS	28" (55CM)
4–6 YRS	30" (76CM)
7–9 YRS	32" (81CM)
10 YRS	34" (86CM)

HAT TO FIT SIZE

SMALL	17" (36CM)
MEDIUM	19" (41CM)
LARGE	21½" (55CM)

YARN

8 (9, 10, 11) skeins Artyarns Supermerino
  #104 variegated blues and greens (MC)

1 skein Artyarns Supermerino
  #120 dark teal (CC)

NEEDLES

size US 9 (5.5mm) needles

size US 7 (4.5mm) needles

16" (40cm) size US 7 (4.5mm) circular needle

16" (40cm) size US 9 (5.5mm) circular needle

size US 9 (5.5mm) dpn

If necessary, change needle size to obtain correct gauge.

NOTIONS

stitch holders

size H (5mm) crochet hook

GAUGE

20 sts and 27 rows = 4" (10cm) on size 9 (5.5mm) needles in stockinette stitch

HAT

With 16" (41cm) size US 9 (5.5mm) circular needle and CC, cast on 84 (96, 108) sts. Work in k2, p2 rib for 7 rows. Change to MC and cont straight in stockinette for 5½ (6½, 7½)" (14[17, 19]cm).

Change to dpn when sts become stretched too far to comfortably knit.

RND 1: * k10, k2tog; rep from * to end of rnd (77 [88, 99] sts).

RND 2: * k9, k2tog; rep from * to end of rnd (70 [80, 90] sts).

RND 3: * k8, k2tog; rep from * to end of rnd (63 [72, 81] sts).

RND 4: * k7, k2tog; rep from * to end of rnd (56 [64, 72] sts).

RND 5: * k6, k2tog; rep from * to end of rnd (49 [56, 63] sts).

RND 6: * k5, k2tog; rep from * to end of rnd (42 [48, 54] sts).

RND 7: * k4, k2tog; rep from * to end of rnd (35 [40, 45] sts).

RND 8: * k3, k2tog; rep from * to end of rnd (28 [32, 36] sts).

RND 9: * k2, k2tog; rep from * to end of rnd (21 [24, 27] sts).

RND 10: * k1, k2tog; rep from * to end of rnd (14 [16, 18] sts).

RND 11: * k2tog; rep from * to end of rnd (7 [8, 9] sts).

Knit 5 (7, 9) rnds with dpn.

Bind off all sts.

SWEATER

BOTTOM PANEL (MAKE 2)

With MC and 16" (40cm) size US 9 (5.5mm) circular needle, CO 20 (20, 25, 25) sts. Work in stockinette until strip measures 14 (15, 16, 17)" (36 [38, 41, 43]cm). Bind off all sts.

BACK

With 16" (40cm) size US 9 (5.5mm) circular needle and CC, with RS facing, pick up and k70 (75, 80, 85) sts across top of one strip. Work 3 rows in stockinette, beg with a purl row.

Change to MC and cont in stockinette until piece measures 10 (10, 12, 12)" (25 [25, 30, 30]cm) from bottom edge of bottom panel.

ARMHOLE SHAPING

Bind off 4 sts at beg of next 2 rows.

NEXT ROW: k2, k2tog, knit to last 4 sts, k2tog tbl, k2.

Working all dec as set, dec 1 st at each end of every alt row 3 times (54 [59, 64, 69] sts). Cont straight until armholes measure 6½ (7, 7½, 8)" (17 [18, 19, 20]cm) ending with a WS row.

SHOULDER AND NECK SHAPING

Bind off 6 (6, 7, 7) sts at beg of next 2 rows.

NEXT ROW: Bind off 6 (6, 6, 7) sts. Work until there are 5 (6, 6, 6) sts on right hand needle. Turn, then bind off rem sts.

Place center 20 (23, 26, 29) sts on a holder. Rejoin yarn and work to end.

NEXT ROW: Bind off 6 (6, 6, 7) sts.

Bind off rem sts.

FRONT

Work front same as back until armholes measure 5 (5½, 6, 6½)" (13 [14, 15, 17]cm), ending with a WS row.

NECK AND SHOULDER SHAPING

k22 (23, 24, 25) sts, turn. Place rem sts on a holder. Dec 1 st at neck edge of next and every foll alt row 4 times (17 [18, 19, 20] sts). Work 2 rows in stockinette. Bind off 6 (6, 7, 7) sts at armhole edge once, then bind off 6 (6, 6, 7) sts at armhole edge once. Bind off rem sts.

SLEEVES

With size US 7 (4.5mm) needles and CC, CO 36 (36, 40, 40) sts. Work in stockinette for 4 rows, then work in k2, p2 rib for 8 (8, 10, 10) rows.

Change to MC and size US 9 (5.5mm) needles. Working in stockinette, inc 1 st at each end of next and every foll sixth (5th, 5th, 5th) row 10 (12, 12, 14) times (58 [62, 66, 70] sts). Cont straight until sleeve measures 12 (13½, 15, 16)" (31 [33, 38, 41]cm) from cast-on edge, ending with a WS row.

Bind off 4 sts at beg of next 2 rows (52 [62, 66, 72] sts). Dec as follows, k2, k2tog, k to last 4 sts, k2tog tbl, k2, at each end of next and every foll alt row 5 (5, 6, 6) times, then every row 14 (16, 16, 18) times 12 [18, 20, 22] sts). Bind off rem sts.

TIP

When knitting with variegated yarn, alternate between two skeins to prevent the colors from pooling.

SHAPE SLEEVE CAPS

Bind off 4 sts at beg of next 2 rows.

NEXT ROW: k2, k2tog, knit to last 4 sts, k2tog tbl, k2.

Working all dec as set, dec 1 st each end of every foll alt row 5 times.

NEXT ROW: p2, p2tog tbl, purl to last 4 sts, p2tog, p2.

NEXT ROW: k2, k2tog, knit to last 4 sts, k2tog tbl, k2.

Working all dec as set, dec 1 st each end of every foll row 12 times (10 [14, 18, 22] sts). Bind off all sts.

FINISHING

Sew shoulder seams.

COLLAR

With RS facing, using 16" (41cm) size US 7 (4.5mm) circular needle and CC, k20 (23, 26, 29) sts from stitch holder at back of neck, pick up and knit 4 sts up left back neck, 13 (14, 13, 14) sts down left front neck, k10 (13, 16, 19) sts from stitch holder at front, pick up and k13 (14, 13, 14) sts up right front neck, and 4 sts down right back neck (64 [72, 76, 84] sts). Work 3 rnds in k2, p2 rib. Knit 2 rows. Bind off loosely.

Sew side and sleeve seams.

With size H crochet hook, work 1 rnd of slip stitch around bottom hem, then 1 round of single crochet. Weave in all ends.

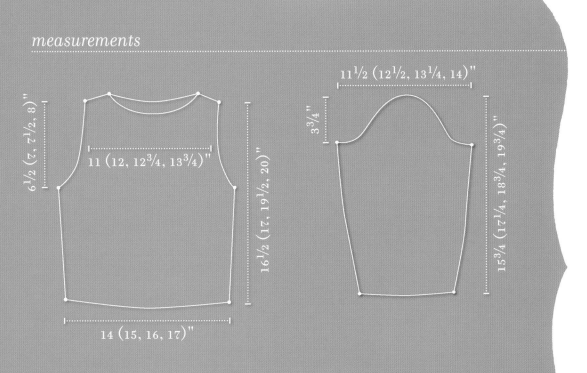

measurements

$6^{1}/_{2}$ (7, $7^{1}/_{2}$, 8)"

11 (12, $12^{3}/_{4}$, $13^{3}/_{4}$)"

$16^{1}/_{2}$ (17, $19^{1}/_{2}$, 20)"

14 (15, 16, 17)"

$11^{1}/_{2}$ ($12^{1}/_{2}$, $13^{1}/_{4}$, 14)"

$3^{3}/_{4}$"

$15^{3}/_{4}$ ($17^{1}/_{4}$, $18^{3}/_{4}$, $19^{3}/_{4}$)"

KNITTING ABBREVIATIONS

alt	ALTERNATE
beg	BEGINNING
BO	BIND OFF
CO	CAST ON
CC	CONTRAST COLOR
cn	CABLE NEEDLE
dec	DECREASE
DPN(s)	DOUBLE-POINTED NEEDLE(S)
est patt	ESTABLISHED PATTERN
foll	FOLLOWING
inc	INCREASE
k	KNIT
k2tog	KNIT 2 TOGETHER
k2tog tbl	KNIT 2 TOGETHER THROUGH BACK LOOP
m1	MAKE ONE INCREASE
MC	MAIN COLOR
p	PURL
p2tog	PURL 2 TOGETHER
p2tog tbl	PURL 2 TOGETHER THROUGH BACK LOOP
p3tog	PURL 3 TOGETHER
pm	PLACE MARKER
psso	PASS SLIPPED STITCH OVER
rem	REMAINING
RS	RIGHT SIDE
rep	REPEAT
sl	SLIP
SSK	SLIP, SLIP, KNIT
st(s)	STITCH(ES)
WS	WRONG SIDE
yds	YARDS
yo	YARN OVER

helpful
INFORMATION

KNITTING NEEDLE CONVERSIONS

diameter (mm)	US size	suggested yarn weight
2	0	LACE WEIGHT
2.25	1	LACE AND FINGERING WEIGHT
2.75	2	LACE AND FINGERING WEIGHT
3.25	3	FINGERING AND SPORT WEIGHT
3.5	4	FINGERING AND SPORT WEIGHT
3.75	5	DK AND SPORT WEIGHT
4	6	DK, SPORT AND ARAN/WORSTED WEIGHT
4.5	7	ARAN/WORSTED WEIGHT
5	8	ARAN/WORSTED AND HEAVY WORSTED WEIGHT
5.5	9	ARAN/WORSTED, HEAVY WORSTED
6	10	CHUNKY/BULKY
6.5	10½	CHUNKY/BULKY AND SUPER BULKY
8	11	CHUNKY/BULKY AND SUPER BULKY
9	13	SUPER BULKY
10	15	SUPER BULKY
12.75	17	SUPER BULKY
15	19	SUPER BULKY
	36	SUPER BULKY

SUBSTITUTING YARNS

At the time of publication, all of the yarns used in this book were still being produced. However, a yarn company may decide to discontinue a particular yarn or color with little or no notice.

When it comes to substituting yarns, gauge is everything. Check the label to make sure that the horizontal gauge (number of stitches per inch) is the same as the required gauge in the pattern that you are working with. To determine yardage, do a web search on the yarn listed in the pattern. Multiply yardage by the number of skeins to determine exactly how much yarn you will need to complete your project. It is best to purchase all of the yarn at once, as it may be difficult to match your dye lot at a later date. Because every knitter knits in a different way, it is always necessary to knit a swatch to determine that you are getting the proper gauge, thus ensuring that the final measurements of your project will be as specified.

CARING FOR YOUR HANDKNITS

HAND-WASHING AND BLOCKING

Handknits should be soaked in cool water with a mild soap. Gently wring and then place on a dry towel and roll out the excess water. Transfer to a dry towel and lay flat to dry. Unless your aim is to stretch your item, you should never hang it to dry. If you are blocking your project to attain a certain measurement, you should pin it to the towel using rust-proof pins. I like to set a fan in front of my blocked project so it dries quicker. Heavy wools take a long time to dry, and if you live in a humid climate they will take even longer. Be sure to change the towel every twelve hours or so on long-drying projects. If your project remains wet for too long, it will begin to smell like laundry that has been left behind in the washer.

STORING YOUR HANDKNITS

Always clean your handknits before storing them, as moths tend to prefer dirty woolens, especially those with food stains. I stopped using mothballs when I discovered that they contain chemicals that can be hazardous to your health. Try storing your handknits with an herb sachet made of lavender, rosemary, cloves or other pungent herbs. Cedar balls and shavings are good, too, but need to be shaved or replaced when they've lost their scent. It is rumored that the solvent used in dry cleaning helps to prevent moths. If you opt to dry clean your projects, you should stick with that. Jumping back and forth between washing and dry cleaning is a no-no, as this tends to break down the fibers, reducing the life of your handknits.

EEK! A MOTH!

If you notice the fibers starting to unravel, chances are a moth has had its way with your stash or your handknits. Place the affected yarn or project in a plastic bag and toss it in the freezer for a day or so. This will kill off any moth larvae and prevent it from doing further damage. I have heard that the microwave also works (minus the plastic bag), but I find the idea a little frightening.

CARE SYMBOLS

Yarn labels can sometimes look like Greek. Here's a quick guide to the symbols you should know the meanings of so you can take good care of your handknits.

Do not wash by hand or machine

Hand washable

Do not press

Machine washable

Do not dry clean

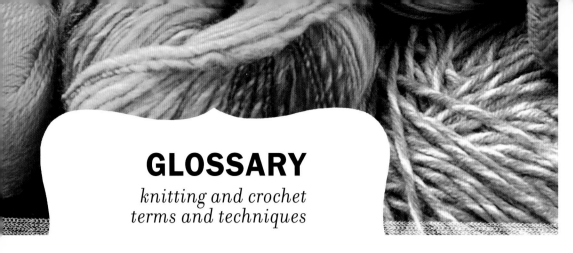

GLOSSARY
knitting and crochet
terms and techniques

CABLES
Although cables may seem difficult, they're really quite simple. To create a cable, slip (sl) the number of stitches indicated in the pattern onto a cable needle (cn) and hold the cable needle at the front or back of the work, as directed. Simply ignore the cable needle and knit the number of stitches indicated in the pattern from the left-hand needle. Rejoin the stitches on the cable needle to the main stitches by knitting them off of the cable needle. Holding the cable needle to the front or back of your work determines the way the cable twists.

CABLE NEEDLE (CN)
A cable needle is a small hook- or U-shaped needle that is pointed on either end. Select a cable needle that is close to the diameter of the needles you use for the project.

CASTING ON (CO)
Casting on is the term for creating the number of stitches needed for the first row of any project. There are several methods for casting on—for the projects in this book, you may use the method you're most comfortable with.

CASTING ON WITH DOUBLE-POINTED NEEDLES
If one of your double-pointed needles can accommodate the full number of stitches, cast all of the stitches onto one needle. If your needles are shorter, you may opt to cast all of the stitches onto

one longer straight needle. Once all of the stitches have been cast on, divide them evenly between four of the dpn. To divide the stitches, hold the needle with the cast-on stitches in your left hand, as if to knit. Using a dpn, insert the tip of the needle into the first stitch as if to purl. Slip the stitch to the right-hand needle. Continue to slip stitches as if to purl until the stitches are divided evenly over four needles. The remaining dpn is for knitting.

CROCHET STITCHES
Some projects in this book use a small crocheted border as a finishing technique. You don't need to know much about crochet; just knowing these basic stitches will do.

SLIP STITCH CROCHET
On right side of fabric, with edge facing away from you, insert hook into top edge of stitch, wrap yarn over hook and pull through fabric. * Insert hook into next stitch, wrap yarn over hook, pull through the fabric and through the loop on hook. Rep from * to create a border as desired.

SINGLE CROCHET
On right side of fabric, with edge facing away from you, insert hook into top edge of stitch, wrap yarn over hook and pull through fabric, wrap yarn over hook and pull through loop. * Insert hook into next stitch, wrap yarn over hook and pull through both loops on hook. Rep from * as desired.

DECREASES

Decreasing is one of the simplest knitting operations to learn. For the projects in this book, decreases are managed by knitting multiple stitches together as one.

KNIT TWO TOGETHER (K2TOG)

Knitting two stitches together as one (k2tog) is a simple way to decrease the number of stitches in a row. Simply slip your right-hand needle through the first two stitches on the left-hand needle, as for a regular knit stitch. Knit the two stitches as one, creating one less stitch.

PURL TWO TOGETHER (P2TOG)

Slip your right-hand needle through the first two stitches on the left-hand needle, as for a regular purl stitch. Purl the two stitches as one, creating one less stitch.

PURL THREE TOGETHER (P3TOG)

Slip your right-hand needle through the first three stitches on the left-hand needle, as for a regular purl stitch. Purl the three stitches as one, decreasing by two stitches.

KNIT OR PURL TWO TOGETHER THROUGH BACK LOOP (K2TOG TBL OR P2TOG TBL)

Insert the right needle into the back loops of the first two stitches on the left-hand needle. Wrap the yarn and knit or purl as usuaL.

SLIP, SLIP, KNIT (SSK)

To create a left-slanting decrease, slip the first stitch as if to knit, slip the second stitch as if to knit, and then bring the right needle through both stitches from front to back and knit them together.

223

INCREASES

There are lots of different ways to increase the number of stitches in a given row. If the pattern simply says inc 1, choose the method of increasing that works best for you.

KNIT ONE IN FRONT AND BACK (KFB)

An easy way to increase is to knit one in the front and back of a stitch (kfb). To make this type of increase, simply insert your right-hand needle into the next stitch on the left-hand needle and knit the stitch, keeping the stitch on the left-hand needle instead of sliding it off. Then bring your right-hand needle around to the back, knit into the back loop of the same stitch, and slip both stitches off the needle. (See Knit One in Front and Back, Fig 1–3.)

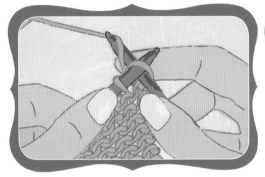

Knit One in Front and Back: Fig 1

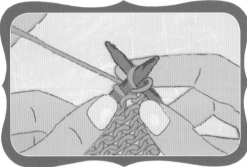

Knit One in Front and Back: Fig 2

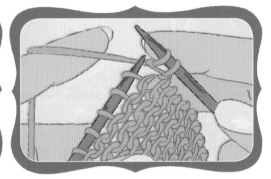

Knit One in Front and Back: Fig 3

MAKE ONE (M1)

With your right-hand needle, pick up the bar between two stitches from the back to front, and place it on the left-hand needle, then knit it through the back loop. (See Make One, Fig 1–2.)

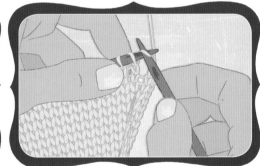

Make One: Fig 1

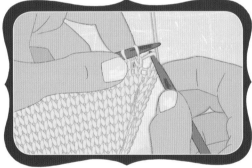

Make One: Fig 2

INTARSIA

At each color change, yarns must be wrapped around each other at the back of the work to prevent holes in the fabric. You may work with separate skeins, with yarn wound on bobbins, or with very long strands of yarn. Take time to untangle your strands every few rows.

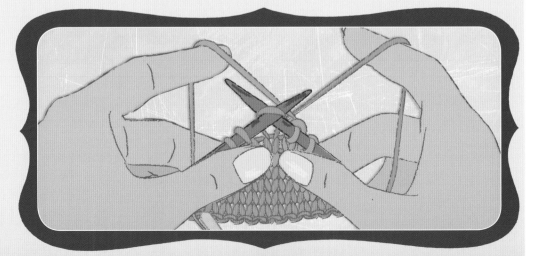

Intarsia

MATTRESS STITCH

Unless otherwise indicated, mattress stitch is used for all seams in this book. Mattress stitch creates an invisible seam by replicating the stitches on either side of the seam using a darning needle and the same yarn used to create the knitted piece.

To create mattress stitch on stockinette pieces, work on the right side of the fabric, bringing the needle up between the two legs of a v stitch on one piece, down through the front of the fabric outside of the v stitch on the other piece of fabric, under both legs of the same stitch, up through the fabric on the other outside of that same stitch, then down through the right side of the first piece of fabric at the same point where you brought the needle up for the first part of the stitch. Repeat along the entire length of the seam. See a reference guide for working mattress stitch on garter stitch. (See Mattress Stitch, Fig 1–4.)

PICKING UP STITCHES

To pick up a stitch, insert the tip of one needle through the side of a stitch from front to back. Leaving about a 3" to 4" (8cm to 10cm) tail, wrap the yarn around the needle as you would for a regular knit stitch. Bring the yarn through the stitch, creating a loop on your needle. This loop is the first picked-up stitch. Continue to pick up the number of stitches required, making sure to space them evenly.

PLACING A MARKER (PM)

Sometimes a pattern calls for you to place a marker (pm). Markers are generally small plastic rings that slide onto a needle and rest in between stitches, marking a certain spot. If you don't have markers on hand, cut small pieces of scrap yarn in a contrasting color. Tie the scrap yarn around the needle in the indicated spot in a loose knot. Move the marker from one needle to the other when you come to it. Continue as usual.

PLACING STITCHES ON A HOLDER

Most sweater patterns require that you place some of the front and back neck stitches onto a holder as you bind off the shoulder stitches. You may buy a stitch holder and slide the stitches onto it, or just use a piece of scrap yarn in a contrasting color. The stitches will be picked back up at the end to make a neckband.

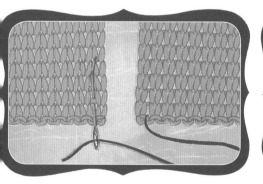

Mattress Stitch: Fig 1

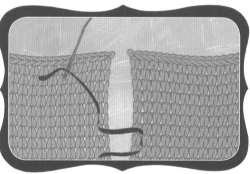

Mattress Stitch: Fig 2

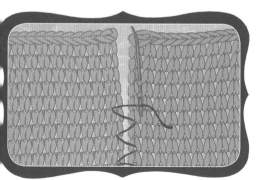

Mattress Stitch: Fig 3

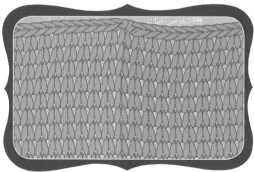

Mattress Stitch: Fig 4

STITCHES

EYELETS

Eyelets are small, decorative holes in knitted fabric. Create them with regular yarn overs. Remember to make an equal number of decreases on the following row so the knitted fabric doesn't grow exponentially.

GARTER STITCH

Garter stitch is created by knitting every row.

GARTER RIDGE

Garter stitch is created by knitting every row. However, if you'd like to add just a bit of texture to punctuate a smoother stitch like stockinette with garter stitch, make sure to knit two rows to create a garter ridge.

RIBBING

To create ribbing, simply alternate between knitting and purling. You can create a one-by-one rib, a two-by-two rib, a one-by-three rib...etc. Ribbing is often used as a border or as trim.

SEED STITCH

Seed stitch is a simple stitch that creates an interesting texture. Seed stitch is worked by knitting all purl stitches and purling all knit stitches. Here's how it works:

FOR AN ODD NUMBER OF STITCHES

ROW 1: * k1, p1; rep from * until last st, k1.

Rep Row 1.

FOR AN EVEN NUMBER OF STITCHES

ROW 1: * k1, p1*, rep from * until end of row.

ROW 2: * p1, k1; rep from * until end of row.

Rep Rows 1–2.

STOCKINETTE STITCH

To create Stockinette stitch, knit on the right side and purl on the wrong side. If you're knitting in the round, knitting every row produces effortless Stockinette with no purling.

YARN OVER (YO)

A yarn over is as easy as it sounds. When you come to a yarn over in the pattern, simply wrap the working yarn around the right-hand needle and continue knitting as usual. On the following row, you will knit or purl the wrapped yarn, creating an extra stitch and also an attractive eyelet hole in the knitted fabric. Because a yarn over creates a new stitch, a row with yarn overs is often combined with decreases.

WHIP STITCH

Fold, at the turning ridge, to the wrong side, lining the edges up evenly. Starting at the corner edge, insert the tapestry needle into a stitch on the wrong side of the fabric and then into the cast-on edge of the fabric that is folded over, and pull the yarn through. Repeat until the end.

WORKING IN THE ROUND

WITH CIRCULAR NEEDLES

Before you begin, make sure that your circular needles are a bit shorter than the diameter of your project. Simply cast on the requisite number of stitches just as you would on straight needles. Also make sure the stitches are not twisted. Hold the needle with the tail dangling from it in your left hand. Push the stitches to the end of the needle. Hold the needle with the working yarn in your right hand, pushing the first stitches to the end of that needle. Insert the tip of the right needle into the first stitch on the left needle from front to back. Wrap the working yarn around the right needle and knit your first stitch. Voilá, you're connected! After that, knit every row to produce Stockinette stitch.

WITH DOUBLE-POINTED NEEDLES

If one of your double-pointed needles can accommodate the full number of stitches, cast all of the stitches onto one needle. If your needles are shorter, you may opt to cast all of the stitches onto one longer straight needle. Once all of the stitches have been cast on, divide them evenly between four of the DPNs. To divide the stitches, hold the needle with the cast-on stitches in your left hand, as if to knit. Using a DPN, insert the tip of the needle into the first stitch as if to purl. Slip the stitch to the right-hand needle. Continue to slip stitches as if to purl until the stitches are divided evenly over four needles. The remaining DPN is for knitting.

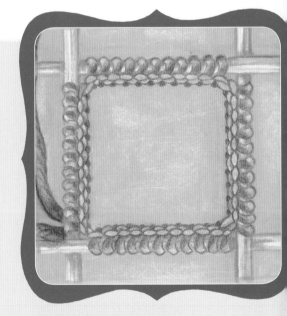

Working in the Round with Double-Pointed Needles

resource
GUIDE

ARTYARNS
39 Westmoreland Avenue
White Plains, NY 10606
914.428.0333
www.artyarns.com

DEBBIE BLISS & NORO YARNS
Distributed by Knitting
Fever International
P.O. Box 336
315 Bayview Avenue
Amityville, NY 11701
516.546.3600
www.knittingfever.com

FILATURA DI CROSA
Distributed by Tahki·Stacy Charles, Inc.
70–30 80th Street, Building 36
Ridgewood, NY 11385
800.338.YARN
www.tahkistacycharles.com

**LANAKNITS DESIGNS
HEMP FOR KNITTING**
Suite 3B, 320 Vernon Street
Nelson BC Canada V1L 4E4
888.301.0011
www.lanaknits.com

LION BRAND YARN CO.
135 Kero Road
Carlstadt, NJ 07072
800.258.YARN
www.lionbrand.com

LORNA'S LACES YARNS
4229 North Honore Street
Chicago, IL 60613
773.995.3803
www.lornaslaces.net

PEACE FLEECE
475 Porterfield Road
Porter, ME 04068
800.482.2841
www.peacefleece.com

ROWAN YARNS
Westminster Fibers, Inc.
165 Ledge Street
Nashua, NH 03063
800.445.9276

**SOUTH WEST TRADING
COMPANY**
918 S. Park Ln., Ste. 102
Tempe, AZ 85281
phone: 480.894.1818

SCOUT'S SWAG
www.scoutsswag.com

knitting
INSPIRATIONS

If you like to knit, it's very likely you enjoy poring over pattern books and magazines, and you may even have discovered the pleasures of the knitting blog. Below are a few of the places I regularly go for knitting inspiration.

MAGAZINES

In the last few years there has been an upsurge in the publication of knitting magazines. If you do a little sleuthing on the Web or a little browsing in your favorite local bookstore, you'll find a wide selection of knitting publications. There's something for every kind of knitting taste and skill level. Here are a few of my favorite knitting mags.

Rowan Magazine
Long an industry standard, Rowan is equally well known for its luxurious yarns and high-fashion knitting patterns. Because of the length of time involved in putting together a knitting publication, it is almost impossible to keep designs current with what is on the runways. Rowan comes closer than most knitting magazines, giving us some of the hottest designs around.

Vintage *Vogue Knitting Magazines* from the 1950s–1960s
What can you say? *Vogue* is always en vogue. Their vintage patterns are painstaking and exquisite (imagine knitting a two piece boucle suit on size 2 needles). Check eBay for vintage editions from the 1940s through the 1960s.

Italian Vogue
For years, *Italian Vogue* has been the ne plus ultra of *Vogue Magazines*. Its cutting-edge fashion and photography sets it miles apart from its competitors. If you want to know what's white hot in fashion, this is where you'll find it!

i-D
This super cool, London-based magazine always has its finger on the pulse of what's new and interesting in art, film, fashion and music worldwide.

KNITTING BOOKS

Knitting books are growing ever more beautiful, entertaining and functional. Every knitter should have a well-rounded selection of books, from the purely inspirational to the practical reference book. Here are a few of the books on my shelves that get repeated thumbing through.

Vogue Knitting: The Ultimate Knitting Book
This reference book is a must-have for every knitter, new and old. From basic beginner's techniques to invaluable information on finishing techniques and advanced knitting skills like colorwork, this book has everything any knitter could need, including in-depth information on correcting your knitting snafus.

Stitch 'N Bitch
BY DEBBIE STOLLER
This fun-to-read book has an extensive how-to knitting guide that even the totally new knitter will find easy to follow. It features hip designs by knitters-turned-designers who are tuned in to what people really want to knit.

The Knitter's Book of Finishing Techniques
BY NANCIE M. WISEMAN
Finishing can make or break a completed project. This excellent reference book provides photos and detailed instructions for a wide variety of finishing techniques.

BLOGS

Watch out, blogs can be dangerously addictive. There's an ever-growing online community of knitters, and they always want to share what's on their needles and what's going on in their lives. Blogs are a great place to get inspiration, patterns and often a few laughs. Here are some of my favorites to visit.

Art for Housewives
WWW.HOUSEWIFE.SPLINDER.COM/
Artist Cynthia Korzekwa devotes this website to her massive compilation of

links to outsider art, recycled craft and domestic arts. If you want to learn how people are reusing, recycling and reinventing, this is the place to go!

Purl Jam
PURLJAM.TYPEPAD.COM
Tracy Stewart, more commonly know to the knitting universe as Rock Chick, is the sassy voice behind this clever knitting blog. Her amusing posts run the gamut from discussing finished and unfinished knitting projects to chronicling her virgin adventure with cleaning raw fleece. Her blog also contains links to some of the coolest knitting on the web.

Strikker
OBSESSIVEKNITTING.BLOGSPOT.COM
It's true. The woman who runs this blog knits obsessively. Go to her blog if you want to a) be inspired or b) be depressed by your own complete lack of productivity.

Mason Dixon Knitting
WWW.MASONDIXONKNITTING.COM
Kay Gardiner and Ann Shayne post back and forth to each other on their blog, bringing warmth and good knitting to the online (and offline) knitting community. They have recently published a knitting book of their own, *Mason-Dixon Knitting*.

Pinku
PINKUROCKS.TYPEPAD.COM/PINKU

Katherine Mok is an Australian knitter living in Tokyo, Japan. As the founder of the Tokyo SnB, she provides an insider's view into the vibrant Tokyo knitting scene. Her blog also features great pictures and stories from her travel adventures.

Knit and Tonic
KNITANDTONIC.TYPEPAD.COM/KNITANDTONIC/
Wendy Bernard of southern California learned to knit when she was eight, but didn't pick up needles again until she was pregnant with her daughter four years ago. Her witty posts and cool projects have won her a devoted following of readers who tune in daily to catch up on her knitting adventures.

Bound by My Hook and Needles Too
WWW.BOUNDBYMYHOOK.BLOGSPOT.COM/
Erica B, a stay-at-home mom from Birmingham, Alabama, is quite the prolific knitter and crocheter. Whether creating her own designs or modifying existing patterns, she whips up more amazingly beautiful projects in a month than I could even dream of. Does this woman ever sleep?

The Sartorialist
WWW.THESARTORIALIST.BLOGSPOT.COM
The mysterious man behind The Sartorialist stops stylish New Yorkers on the street and asks if he can photograph

them. The result: Daily photos of some of the most creative and innovative dressers in the world.

WEB SITES
There are all sorts of knit-centric Web sites out there now, as well as tons of non-knitting sites from which to draw great inspiration. Here are a few I visit often.

Camilla Engman
WWW.CAMILLAENGMAN.COM
Camilla Engman is a Swedish artist and crocheter whose whimsical work always makes me look for a way to introduce a bit more humor into my designs. Her highly sought after crocheted characters are an absolute delight!

The Quilts of Gee's Bend
WWW.QUILTSOFGEESBEND.COM/QUILTS/
The astounding work of the Gee's Bend Quilters is the foundation for my design and color aesthetic. Their handiwork, as well as their personal stories, come together to create a rich tapestry of inspiration. Seeing the beauty they produce using limited materials is sure to serve as motivation to create something from even the smallest stash!

Whip Up
WWW.WHIPUP.NET
Whip Up is a collective of artists and crafters from around the world who post daily on everything craft. From knitting

home decor INSPIRATION

Since this book is as much about decorating your home as it is about knitting, I thought I'd share some of the resources I use to get inspiration for styling my space. These magazines and Web sites will start you daydreaming about how you can make your home the best reflection of you.

MAGAZINES

There is no shortage of home decor magazines on the market today! From DIY to "Darling, let's ring up the decorator," there are magazines to fit every budget, taste and lifestyle imaginable. I also find architecture magazines very inspiring. Impeccably styled, they give me great ideas on how to arrange furniture and accessories.

DOMINO MAGAZINE

Every month I eagerly await the arrival of this magazine. Every issue is overflowing with beautiful goodies for the home. From pricey one-of-a-kind *objets d'art* to cool furniture available at big-name bargain stores, *Domino* is full of loads of great must-haves and interesting decorating ideas. My favorite section is "Editors' Cravings," where a theme is chosen, such as "60s Jet Set" or "Jazz Age Finery," and *Domino* editors pick some of their favorite finds that reflect the stated theme.

DWELL MAGAZINE

While *Dwell* is more of an architecture and design mag, it does a beautiful job when it comes to styling living spaces. From grass-covered houses to famed architect Philip Johnson's Glass House, you are sure to be intrigued. If you want a glimpse into the genius behind some of the most original homes in America, you will definitely want to give *Dwell* a gander.

OBJEKT INTERNATIONAL

Objekt International is a beautiful quarterly magazine devoted to interiors, architecture, gardens, art, antiques and design. Each issue is an essential reference piece for people who are seeking creative ideas for living. Their features on some of the most innovative and creative minds in the world, such as designer Veronica Etro, are truly awe-inspiring!

BLOGS AND WEB SITES

There are the people who make things, and there are the people who style things that other people make. In other words, they tell you where to place them in a room and how to get them to play nicely with the rest of the decor. This list primarily features the latter. Why? Because you already know how to knit unique and beautiful accessories for your home. Here's a little help just in case you are not sure where to put them or how to make them work with everything else!

APARTMENT THERAPY

http://www.apartmenttherapy.com/

The Apartment Therapy blog features product reviews, furniture classifieds and helpful Q&A, such as: "How do you hang curtains on a corner window?" It also hosts an annual Smallest Coolest Apartment contest. If you live in a small space, you will love the great ideas you find here!

DECOR8

http://decor8.blogspot.com/

Decor8 bills itself as "a quick fix for design addicts who love decorating their homes but find it challenging to shop online." This fabulous blog provides readers with product and shop reviews and alerts readers to sales and bargain finds. It also lists a design blog and a design book of the week. And there's more! The site features interviews with some of the most innovative minds working in craft and design.

DESIGNER'S LIBRARY

http://designerslibrary.typepad.com/

I am in love with Meg Mateo Ilasco's blog, Designer's Library. She has fantastic taste and a great eye for design. She posts pics from inspiring vintage design books and magazines, as well as offers features on fabulous new designers. If you are looking for an original idea on how to style your living space, this is the place to go!

DESIGN*SPONGE

http://designsponge.blogspot.com/

Grace Bonney of Design*Sponge definitely has her finger on the pulse of what's happening in the worlds of art, craft and design. Her up-to-the-minute reports on all things stylish keep me informed on the latest trends, ideas and products making waves worldwide.

STYLE COURT

http://stylecourt.blogspot.com

The savvy woman behind Style Court definitely knows her stuff. This is the place to go if you want to educate yourself on classic interior design and decorative arts. Her posts are well-researched, informative and inspiring.

INDEX

check out these other fabulous
KNITTING AND CROCHET TITLES
FROM NORTH LIGHT BOOKS.

DomiKNITrix
BY JENNIFER STAFFORD

Once you know the joys of disciplined knitting, you'll never look back. Let experienced knitter Jennifer Stafford help you whip your stitches into shape. This book features a no-nonsense, comprehensive guide to essential knitting operations and finishing techniques. In the second half of the book, you'll put your knitting know-how to the test with patterns for over 20 handknit projects to wear and gift, including a halter "bra-let," a contoured zipper vest, a Jughead hat, icon sweaters and even a knitted mohawk. Plus much, much more.

ISBN-13: 978-1-58180-853-7
ISBN-10: 1-58180-853-4
FLEXIBIND CASE, 240 PAGES, Z0171

Crochet Squared
BY MARSHA A. POLK

If you can crochet a simple scarf, you can make any of the stylish and sophisticated body wraps and accessories featured in *Crochet Squared*. Each of the over 20 projects in the book is based on a simple square or rectangle shape, allowing even beginning crocheters to make gorgeous works of art. *Crochet Squared* takes crochet out of the time warp and brings it into the new millennium. Marsha Polk's striking use of color and novelty yarns makes these for stunning and sophisticated projects. You'll also find a practical guide to basic crochet techniques.

ISBN-13: 978-1-58180-833-9
ISBN-10: 1-58180-833-X
PAPERBACK, 128 PAGES, 33507

Knitter's Bible: Knitted Accessories
BY CLAIRE CROMPTON

This collection of over 30 stylish knitted accessories for every season is sure to please knitters of all skill levels. Projects range from simple scarves and mittens to eye-catching hats and ponchos. With easy-to-follow techniques, detailed photography and plenty of variations, this guide is a must-have for knitters who want to create their own accessories or give a personalized gift.

ISBN-13: 978-0-7153-2327-4
ISBN-10: 0-7153-2327-X
PAPERBACK, 128 PAGES, Z0465

Fitted Knits
BY STEFANIE JAPEL

Fitted Knits features 25 projects to fit and flatter. You'll learn how to tailor T-shirts, sweaters, cardigans, coats and even a skirt and a dress to fit you perfectly. Take the guesswork out of knitting garments that fit. The book includes a detailed section that shows you how to know when and where increases and decreases should be placed to create the most attractive shaping.

ISBN-13: 978-1-58180-872-8
ISBN-10: 1-58180-872-0
PAPERBACK, 144 PAGES, Z0574

These and other fine North Light titles are available at your local craft retailer or bookstore, at www.fwbookstore.com or from other online suppliers.